# REVISED MARPOL ANNEX VI

REGULATIONS FOR THE PREVENTION OF AIR POLLUTION FROM SHIPS

AND

# $NO_x$ Technical Code 2008

2009 Edition

London, 2009

*Published by the*
INTERNATIONAL MARITIME ORGANIZATION
4 Albert Embankment, London SE1 7SR
www.imo.org

*Second edition, 2009*

Printed and bound by CPI Group (UK) Ltd, Croydon, CR0 4YY

ISBN: 978-92-801-4243-3

| IMO PUBLICATION |
|---|
| Sales number: IA664E |



023134

# Contents

# Foreword

In the late 1980s, the International Maritime Organization (IMO) started work on prevention of air pollution from ships. These efforts were based on scientific information on adverse effects of emissions to air from a multitude of sources, ships being one of them, on vulnerable ecosystems. This was something of a departure, as IMO's focus, along with that of national regulators and of society as a whole, had previously been on more visible sources of ship-sourced pollution – for example, on oil spills resulting from major ship accidents. The harmful long-term effects of ships' exhaust gases on human health and the environment were not so immediately visible and had not earlier been fully recognized.

The seventeenth session of the IMO Assembly, in November 1991, recognizing the urgent necessity of establishing an international policy on prevention of air pollution from ships, considered and decided, in resolution A.719(17), to develop a new annex to the International Convention for the Prevention of Pollution from Ships, 1973, as modified by the Protocol of 1978 (MARPOL Convention).

Following development of the regulatory text by IMO's Marine Environment Protection Committee (MEPC), an International Conference of Parties to the MARPOL Convention was held in London from 15 to 26 September 1997. The Conference adopted the Protocol of 1997 to the MARPOL Convention, which added a new Annex VI, Regulations for the Prevention of Air Pollution from Ships, to the MARPOL Convention (MARPOL Annex VI). The Conference also adopted, by Conference resolution 2, the Technical Code on Control of Emission of Nitrogen Oxides from Marine Diesel Engines ($NO_x$ Technical Code), which is mandatory under MARPOL Annex VI.

The 1997 Air Pollution Conference was a historic response by IMO to the need to minimize emissions from ships and their contribution to global air pollution and environmental problems. With the objective of achieving the desired reduction of $NO_x$ in the future, the 1997 Conference requested that the MEPC review the $NO_x$ emission limits at a minimum of five-year intervals after the entry into force of MARPOL Annex VI, and amend them as appropriate.

Following the entry into force of MARPOL Annex VI on 19 May 2005, MEPC 53 (July 2005) agreed to the revision of MARPOL Annex VI and the $NO_x$ Technical Code with the aim of significantly strengthening the emission limits in light of technological improvements and implementation experience, and then instructed the IMO Sub-Committee on Bulk Liquids and Gases to prepare the draft amendments to MARPOL Annex VI and $NO_x$ Technical Code. As a result, MEPC 58 (October 2008) considered and adopted the revised MARPOL Annex VI and the $NO_x$ Technical Code 2008, which are expected to enter into force on 1 July 2010 upon their deemed acceptance on 1 January 2010.

This publication contains the revised MARPOL Annex VI and the $NO_x$ Technical Code 2008, as well as additional information relevant to the prevention of air pollution from ships.

A number of guidelines and other non-mandatory instruments will be developed or updated as a consequence of the revision of MARPOL Annex VI and the $NO_x$ Technical Code. These guidelines and other non-mandatory instruments will be published in a separate publication in 2010. For further information, see the Future developments section of this book.

# REVISED MARPOL ANNEX VI

## Regulations for the Prevention of Air Pollution from Ships

## Revised MARPOL Annex VI
*Regulations for the Prevention of Air Pollution from Ships*

# Contents

APPENDICES

## Resolution MEPC.176(58)

*(adopted on 10 October 2008)*

# AMENDMENTS TO THE ANNEX OF THE PROTOCOL OF 1997 TO AMEND THE INTERNATIONAL CONVENTION FOR THE PREVENTION OF POLLUTION FROM SHIPS, 1973, AS MODIFIED BY THE PROTOCOL OF 1978 RELATING THERETO (Revised MARPOL Annex VI)

THE MARINE ENVIRONMENT PROTECTION COMMITTEE,

RECALLING Article 38(a) of the Convention on the International Maritime Organization concerning the functions of the Marine Environment Protection Committee (the Committee) conferred upon it by international conventions for the prevention and control of marine pollution,

NOTING article 16 of the International Convention for the Prevention of Pollution from Ships, 1973 (hereinafter referred to as the "1973 Convention"), article VI of the Protocol of 1978 relating to the International Convention for the Prevention of Pollution from Ships, 1973 (hereinafter referred to as the "1978 Protocol") and article 4 of the Protocol of 1997 to amend the International Convention for the Prevention of Pollution from Ships, 1973, as modified by the Protocol of 1978 relating thereto (herein after referred to as the "1997 Protocol"), which together specify the amendment procedure of the 1997 Protocol and confer upon the appropriate body of the Organization the function of considering and adopting amendments to the 1973 Convention, as modified by the 1978 and 1997 Protocols,

NOTING ALSO that, by the 1997 Protocol, Annex VI entitled Regulations for the Prevention of Air Pollution from Ships is added to the 1973 Convention (hereinafter referred to as "Annex VI"),

HAVING CONSIDERED the draft amendments to MARPOL Annex VI,

1. ADOPTS, in accordance with article 16(2)(d) of the 1973 Convention, the amendments to Annex VI, the text of which is set out at Annex to the present resolution;

2. DETERMINES, in accordance with article 16(2)(f)(iii) of the 1973 Convention, that the amendments shall be deemed to have been accepted on 1 January 2010, unless prior to that date, not less than one-third of the Parties or Parties the combined merchant fleets of which constitute not less than 50 per cent of the gross tonnage of the world's merchant fleet, have communicated to the Organization their objection to the amendments;

3. INVITES the Parties to note that, in accordance with article 16(2)(g)(ii) of the 1973 Convention, the said amendments shall enter into force on 1 July 2010 upon their acceptance in accordance with paragraph 2 above;

4. REQUESTS the Secretary-General, in conformity with article 16(2)(e) of the 1973 Convention, to transmit to all Parties to the 1973 Convention, as modified by the 1978 and 1997 Protocols, certified copies of the present resolution and the text of the amendments contained in the Annex;

5. REQUESTS FURTHER the Secretary-General to transmit to the Members of the Organization which are not Parties to the 1973 Convention, as modified by the 1978 and 1997 Protocols, copies of the present resolution and its Annex; and

6. INVITES the Parties to MARPOL Annex VI and other Member Governments to bring the amendments to MARPOL Annex VI to the attention of shipowners, ship operators, shipbuilders, marine diesel engine manufacturers, marine fuel suppliers and any other interested groups.

# Regulations for the Prevention of Air Pollution from Ships

## Chapter 1
*General*

### Regulation 1
*Application*
The provisions of this Annex shall apply to all ships, except where expressly provided otherwise in regulations 3, 5, 6, 13, 15, 16 and 18 of this Annex.

### Regulation 2
*Definitions*

For the purpose of this Annex:

**1** *Annex* means Annex VI to the International Convention for the Prevention of Pollution from Ships, 1973 (MARPOL), as modified by the Protocol of 1978 relating thereto (MARPOL 73/78), and as modified by the Protocol of 1997, as amended by the Organization, provided that such amendments are adopted and brought into force in accordance with the provisions of article 16 of the present Convention.

**2** *A similar stage of construction* means the stage at which:

**.1** construction identifiable with a specific ship begins; and

**.2** assembly of that ship has commenced comprising at least 50 tonnes or one per cent of the estimated mass of all structural material, whichever is less.

**3** *Anniversary date* means the day and the month of each year that will correspond to the date of expiry of the International Air Pollution Prevention Certificate.

**4** *Auxiliary control device* means a system, function or control strategy installed on a marine diesel engine that is used to protect the engine and/or its ancillary equipment against operating conditions that could result in damage or failure, or that is used to facilitate the starting of the engine. An auxiliary control device may also be a strategy or measure that has been satisfactorily demonstrated not to be a defeat device.

**5** *Continuous feeding* is defined as the process whereby waste is fed into a combustion chamber without human assistance while the incinerator is in normal operating conditions with the combustion chamber operative temperature between 850°C and 1200°C.

**6** *Defeat device* means a device that measures, senses or responds to operating variables (e.g., engine speed, temperature, intake pressure or any other parameter) for the purpose of activating, modulating, delaying or deactivating the operation of any component or the function of the emission control system such that the effectiveness of the emission control system is reduced under conditions encountered during normal operation, unless the use of such a device is substantially included in the applied emission certification test procedures.

**7** *Emission* means any release of substances, subject to control by this Annex, from ships into the atmosphere or sea.

**8** *Emission control area* means an area where the adoption of special mandatory measures for emissions from ships is required to prevent, reduce and control air pollution from $NO_x$ or $SO_x$ and particulate matter or all three types of emissions and their attendant adverse impacts on human health and the environment. Emission control areas shall include those listed in, or designated under, regulations 13 and 14 of this Annex.

**9** *Fuel oil* means any fuel delivered to and intended for combustion purposes for propulsion or operation on board a ship, including distillate and residual fuels.

**10** *Gross tonnage* means the gross tonnage calculated in accordance with the tonnage measurement regulations contained in Annex I to the International Convention on Tonnage Measurements of Ships, 1969, or any successor Convention.

**11** *Installations* in relation to regulation 12 of this Annex means the installation of systems, equipment, including portable fire-extinguishing units, insulation, or other material on a ship, but excludes the repair or recharge of previously installed systems, equipment, insulation or other material, or the recharge of portable fire-extinguishing units.

**12** *Installed* means a marine diesel engine that is or is intended to be fitted on a ship, including a portable auxiliary marine diesel engine, only if its fuelling, cooling or exhaust system is an integral part of the ship. A fuelling system is considered integral to the ship only if it is permanently affixed to the ship. This definition includes a marine diesel engine that is used to supplement or augment the installed power capacity of the ship and is intended to be an integral part of the ship.

**13** *Irrational emission control strategy* means any strategy or measure that, when the ship is operated under normal conditions of use, reduces the effectiveness of an emission control system to a level below that expected on the applicable emission test procedures.

**14** *Marine diesel engine* means any reciprocating internal combustion engine operating on liquid or dual fuel, to which regulation 13 of this Annex applies, including booster/compound systems if applied.

**15** *$NO_x$ Technical Code* means the Technical Code on Control of Emission of Nitrogen Oxides from Marine Diesel Engines adopted by resolution 2 of the 1997 MARPOL Conference, as amended by the Organization, provided that such amendments are adopted and brought into force in accordance with the provisions of article 16 of the present Convention.

**16** *Ozone-depleting substances* means controlled substances defined in paragraph (4) of article 1 of the Montreal Protocol on Substances that Deplete the Ozone Layer, 1987, listed in Annexes A, B, C or E to the said Protocol in force at the time of application or interpretation of this Annex.

Ozone-depleting substances that may be found on board ship include, but are not limited to:

| | |
|---|---|
| Halon 1211 | Bromochlorodifluoromethane |
| Halon 1301 | Bromotrifluoromethane |
| Halon 2402 | 1,2-Dibromo-1,1,2,2-tetraflouroethane (also known as Halon 114B2) |
| CFC-11 | Trichlorofluoromethane |
| CFC-12 | Dichlorodifluoromethane |
| CFC-113 | 1,1,2-Trichloro-1,2,2-trifluoroethane |
| CFC-114 | 1,2-Dichloro-1,1,2,2-tetrafluoroethane |
| CFC-115 | Chloropentafluoroethane |

**17** *Shipboard incineration* means the incineration of wastes or other matter on board a ship, if such wastes or other matter were generated during the normal operation of that ship.

**18** *Shipboard incinerator* means a shipboard facility designed for the primary purpose of incineration.

**19** *Ships constructed* means ships the keels of which are laid or that are at a similar stage of construction.

**20** *Sludge oil* means sludge from the fuel oil or lubricating oil separators, waste lubricating oil from main or auxiliary machinery, or waste oil from bilge water separators, oil filtering equipment or drip trays.

**21** *Tanker* means an oil tanker as defined in regulation 1 of Annex I or a chemical tanker as defined in regulation 1 of Annex II of the present Convention.

## Regulation 3
*Exceptions and exemptions*

### General

**1** Regulations of this Annex shall not apply to:

- **.1** any emission necessary for the purpose of securing the safety of a ship or saving life at sea; or
- **.2** any emission resulting from damage to a ship or its equipment:
  - **.2.1** provided that all reasonable precautions have been taken after the occurrence of the damage or discovery of the emission for the purpose of preventing or minimizing the emission; and
  - **.2.2** except if the owner or the master acted either with intent to cause damage, or recklessly and with knowledge that damage would probably result.

### Trials for ship emission reduction and control technology research

**2** The Administration of a Party may, in co-operation with other Administrations as appropriate, issue an exemption from specific provisions of this Annex for a ship to conduct trials for the development of ship emission reduction and control technologies and engine design programmes. Such an exemption shall only be provided if the applications of specific provisions of the Annex or the revised $NO_x$ Technical Code 2008 could impede research into the development of such technologies or programmes. A permit for such an exemption shall only be provided to the minimum number of ships necessary and be subject to the following provisions:

**.1** for marine diesel engines with a per cylinder displacement up to 30 litres, the duration of the sea trial shall not exceed 18 months. If additional time is required, a permitting Administration or Administrations may permit a renewal for one additional 18-month period; or

**.2** for marine diesel engines with a per cylinder displacement at or above 30 litres, the duration of the ship trial shall not exceed 5 years and shall require a progress review by the permitting Administration or Administrations at each intermediate survey. A permit may be withdrawn based on this review if the testing has not adhered to the conditions of the permit or if it is determined that the technology or programme is not likely to produce effective results in the reduction and control of ship emissions. If the reviewing Administration or Administrations determine that additional time is required to conduct a test of a particular technology or programme, a permit may be renewed for an additional time period not to exceed five years.

## Emissions from sea-bed mineral activities

**3.1** Emissions directly arising from the exploration, exploitation and associated offshore processing of sea-bed mineral resources are, consistent with article 2(3)(b)(ii) of the present Convention, exempt from the provisions of this Annex. Such emissions include the following:

**.1** emissions resulting from the incineration of substances that are solely and directly the result of exploration, exploitation and associated offshore processing of sea-bed mineral resources, including but not limited to the flaring of hydrocarbons and the burning of cuttings, muds, and/or stimulation fluids during well completion and testing operations, and flaring arising from upset conditions;

**.2** the release of gases and volatile compounds entrained in drilling fluids and cuttings;

**.3** emissions associated solely and directly with the treatment, handling or storage of sea-bed minerals; and

**.4** emissions from marine diesel engines that are solely dedicated to the exploration, exploitation and associated offshore processing of sea-bed mineral resources.

**3.2** The requirements of regulation 18 of this Annex shall not apply to the use of hydrocarbons that are produced and subsequently used on site as fuel, when approved by the Administration.

## Regulation 4
*Equivalents*

**1** The Administration of a Party may allow any fitting, material, appliance or apparatus to be fitted in a ship or other procedures, alternative fuel oils, or compliance methods used as an alternative to that required by this Annex if such fitting, material, appliance or apparatus or other procedures, alternative fuel oils, or compliance methods are at least as effective in terms of emissions reductions as that required by this Annex, including any of the standards set forth in regulations 13 and 14.

**2** The Administration of a Party that allows a fitting, material, appliance or apparatus or other procedures, alternative fuel oils, or compliance methods used as an alternative to that required by this Annex shall communicate to the Organization for circulation to the Parties particulars thereof, for their information and appropriate action, if any.

**3** The Administration of a Party should take into account any relevant guidelines developed by the Organization pertaining to the equivalents provided for in this regulation.

**4** The Administration of a Party that allows the use of an equivalent as set forth in paragraph 1 of this regulation shall endeavour not to impair or damage its environment, human health, property or resources or those of other States.

# Chapter 2

*Survey, certification and means of control*

## Regulation 5

*Surveys*

**1** Every ship of 400 gross tonnage and above and every fixed and floating drilling rig and other platforms shall be subject to the surveys specified below:

**.1** An initial survey before the ship is put into service or before the certificate required under regulation 6 of this Annex is issued for the first time. This survey shall be such as to ensure that the equipment, systems, fittings, arrangements and material fully comply with the applicable requirements of this Annex;

**.2** A renewal survey at intervals specified by the Administration, but not exceeding five years, except where regulation 9.2, 9.5, 9.6 or 9.7 of this Annex is applicable. The renewal survey shall be such as to ensure that the equipment, systems, fittings, arrangements and material fully comply with applicable requirements of this Annex;

**.3** An intermediate survey within three months before or after the second anniversary date or within three months before or after the third anniversary date of the certificate, which shall take the place of one of the annual surveys specified in paragraph 1.4 of this regulation. The intermediate survey shall be such as to ensure that the equipment and arrangements fully comply with the applicable requirements of this Annex and are in good working order. Such intermediate surveys shall be endorsed on the certificate issued under regulation 6 or 7 of this Annex;

**.4** An annual survey within three months before or after each anniversary date of the certificate, including a general inspection of the equipment, systems, fittings, arrangements and material referred to in paragraph 1.1 of this regulation to ensure that they have been maintained in accordance with paragraph 4 of this regulation and that they remain satisfactory for the service for which the ship is intended.

Such annual surveys shall be endorsed on the certificate issued under regulation 6 or 7 of this Annex; and

**.5** An additional survey either general or partial, according to the circumstances, shall be made whenever any important repairs or renewals are made as prescribed in paragraph 4 of this regulation or after a repair resulting from investigations prescribed in paragraph 5 of this regulation. The survey shall be such as to ensure that the necessary repairs or renewals have been effectively made, that the material and workmanship of such repairs or renewals are in all respects satisfactory and that the ship complies in all respects with the requirements of this Annex.

**2** In the case of ships of less than 400 gross tonnage, the Administration may establish appropriate measures in order to ensure that the applicable provisions of this Annex are complied with.

**3** Surveys of ships as regards the enforcement of the provisions of this Annex shall be carried out by officers of the Administration.

**.1** The Administration may, however, entrust the surveys either to surveyors nominated for the purpose or to organizations recognized by it. Such organizations shall comply with the guidelines adopted by the Organization;*

**.2** The survey of marine diesel engines and equipment for compliance with regulation 13 of this Annex shall be conducted in accordance with the revised $NO_x$ Technical Code 2008;

**.3** When a nominated surveyor or recognized organization determines that the condition of the equipment does not correspond substantially with the particulars of the certificate, it shall ensure that corrective action is taken and shall in due course notify the Administration. If such corrective action is not taken, the certificate shall be withdrawn by the Administration. If the ship is in a port of another Party, the appropriate authorities of the port State shall also be notified

* Refer to the Guidelines for the authorization of organizations acting on behalf of the Administration, adopted by the Organization by resolution A.739(18), as may be amended by the Organization, and the Specifications on the survey and certification functions of recognized organizations acting on behalf of the Administration, adopted by the Organization by resolution A.789(19), as may be amended by the Organization.

immediately. When an officer of the Administration, a nominated surveyor or recognized organization has notified the appropriate authorities of the port State, the Government of the port State concerned shall give such officer, surveyor or organization any necessary assistance to carry out their obligations under this regulation; and

**.4** In every case, the Administration concerned shall fully guarantee the completeness and efficiency of the survey and shall undertake to ensure the necessary arrangements to satisfy this obligation.

**4** The equipment shall be maintained to conform with the provisions of this Annex and no changes shall be made in the equipment, systems, fittings, arrangements or material covered by the survey, without the express approval of the Administration. The direct replacement of such equipment and fittings with equipment and fittings that conform with the provisions of this Annex is permitted.

**5** Whenever an accident occurs to a ship or a defect is discovered that substantially affects the efficiency or completeness of its equipment covered by this Annex, the master or owner of the ship shall report at the earliest opportunity to the Administration, a nominated surveyor or recognized organization responsible for issuing the relevant certificate.

## Regulation 6

*Issue or endorsement of a Certificate*

**1** An International Air Pollution Prevention Certificate shall be issued, after an initial or renewal survey in accordance with the provisions of regulation 5 of this Annex, to:

**.1** any ship of 400 gross tonnage and above engaged in voyages to ports or offshore terminals under the jurisdiction of other Parties; and

**.2** platforms and drilling rigs engaged in voyages to waters under the sovereignty or jurisdiction of other Parties.

**2** A ship constructed before the date of entry into force of Annex VI for such ship's Administration shall be issued with an International Air Pollution Prevention Certificate in accordance with paragraph 1 of this regulation no later than the first scheduled dry-docking after the date of such entry into force, but in no case later than three years after this date.

**3** Such certificate shall be issued or endorsed either by the Administration or by any person or organization duly authorized by it. In every case, the Administration assumes full responsibility for the certificate.

## Regulation 7
*Issue of a Certificate by another Party*

**1** A Party may, at the request of the Administration, cause a ship to be surveyed and, if satisfied that the provisions of this Annex are complied with, shall issue or authorize the issuance of an International Air Pollution Prevention Certificate to the ship, and where appropriate, endorse or authorize the endorsement of that certificate on the ship, in accordance with this Annex.

**2** A copy of the certificate and a copy of the survey report shall be transmitted as soon as possible to the requesting Administration.

**3** A certificate so issued shall contain a statement to the effect that it has been issued at the request of the Administration and it shall have the same force and receive the same recognition as a certificate issued under regulation 6 of this Annex.

**4** No International Air Pollution Prevention Certificate shall be issued to a ship that is entitled to fly the flag of a State which is not a Party.

## Regulation 8
*Form of Certificate*

The International Air Pollution Prevention Certificate shall be drawn up in a form corresponding to the model given in appendix I to this Annex and shall be at least in English, French or Spanish. If an official language of the issuing country is also used, this shall prevail in case of a dispute or discrepancy.

## Regulation 9
*Duration and validity of Certificate*

**1** An International Air Pollution Prevention Certificate shall be issued for a period specified by the Administration, which shall not exceed five years.

**2** Notwithstanding the requirements of paragraph 1 of this regulation:

**.1** when the renewal survey is completed within three months before the expiry date of the existing certificate, the new certificate shall be valid from the date of completion of the renewal survey to a date not exceeding five years from the date of expiry of the existing certificate;

**.2** when the renewal survey is completed after the expiry date of the existing certificate, the new certificate shall be valid from the date of completion of the renewal survey to a date not exceeding five years from the date of expiry of the existing certificate; and

**.3** when the renewal survey is completed more than three months before the expiry date of the existing certificate, the new certificate shall be valid from the date of completion of the renewal survey to a date not exceeding five years from the date of completion of the renewal survey.

**3** If a certificate is issued for a period of less than five years, the Administration may extend the validity of the certificate beyond the expiry date to the maximum period specified in paragraph 1 of this regulation, provided that the surveys referred to in regulations 5.1.3 and 5.1.4 of this Annex applicable when a certificate is issued for a period of five years are carried out as appropriate.

**4** If a renewal survey has been completed and a new certificate cannot be issued or placed on board the ship before the expiry date of the existing certificate, the person or organization authorized by the Administration may endorse the existing certificate and such a certificate shall be accepted as valid for a further period that shall not exceed five months from the expiry date.

**5** If a ship, at the time when a certificate expires, is not in a port in which it is to be surveyed, the Administration may extend the period of validity of the certificate, but this extension shall be granted only for the purpose of allowing the ship to complete its voyage to the port in which it is to be surveyed, and then only in cases where it appears proper and reasonable to do so. No certificate shall be extended for a period longer than three months, and a ship to which an extension is granted shall not, on its arrival in the port in which it is to be surveyed, be entitled by virtue of such extension to leave that port without having a new certificate. When the renewal survey is completed, the new certificate shall be valid to a date not exceeding five years from the date of expiry of the existing certificate before the extension was granted.

**6** A certificate issued to a ship engaged on short voyages that has not been extended under the foregoing provisions of this regulation may be extended by the Administration for a period of grace of up to one month from the date of expiry stated on it. When the renewal survey is completed, the new certificate shall be valid to a date not exceeding five years from the date of expiry of the existing certificate before the extension was granted.

**7** In special circumstances, as determined by the Administration, a new certificate need not be dated from the date of expiry of the existing certificate as required by paragraph 2.1, 5 or 6 of this regulation. In these special circumstances, the new certificate shall be valid to a date not exceeding five years from the date of completion of the renewal survey.

**8** If an annual or intermediate survey is completed before the period specified in regulation 5 of this Annex, then:

- **.1** the anniversary date shown on the certificate shall be amended by endorsement to a date that shall not be more than three months later than the date on which the survey was completed;
- **.2** the subsequent annual or intermediate survey required by regulation 5 of this Annex shall be completed at the intervals prescribed by that regulation using the new anniversary date; and
- **.3** the expiry date may remain unchanged, provided one or more annual or intermediate surveys, as appropriate, are carried out so that the maximum intervals between the surveys prescribed by regulation 5 of this Annex are not exceeded.

**9** A certificate issued under regulation 6 or 7 of this Annex shall cease to be valid in any of the following cases:

- **.1** if the relevant surveys are not completed within the periods specified under regulation 5.1 of this Annex;
- **.2** if the certificate is not endorsed in accordance with regulation 5.1.3 or 5.1.4 of this Annex; and
- **.3** upon transfer of the ship to the flag of another State. A new certificate shall only be issued when the Government issuing the new certificate is fully satisfied that the ship is in compliance with the requirements of regulation 5.4 of this Annex. In the case of a transfer between Parties, if requested within three months after the transfer has taken place, the Government of the Party whose flag the ship was formerly entitled to fly shall, as soon as possible, transmit to the Administration copies of the certificate carried by the ship before the transfer and, if available, copies of the relevant survey reports.

## Regulation 10

*Port State control on operational requirements*

**1** A ship, when in a port or an offshore terminal under the jurisdiction of another Party, is subject to inspection by officers duly authorized by such Party concerning operational requirements under this Annex, where there are clear grounds for believing that the master or crew are not familiar with essential shipboard procedures relating to the prevention of air pollution from ships.

**2** In the circumstances given in paragraph 1 of this regulation, the Party shall take such steps as to ensure that the ship shall not sail until the situation has been brought to order in accordance with the requirements of this Annex.

**3** Procedures relating to the port State control prescribed in article 5 of the present Convention shall apply to this regulation.

**4** Nothing in this regulation shall be construed to limit the rights and obligations of a Party carrying out control over operational requirements specifically provided for in the present Convention.

## Regulation 11

*Detection of violations and enforcement*

**1** Parties shall co-operate in the detection of violations and the enforcement of the provisions of this Annex, using all appropriate and practicable measures of detection and environmental monitoring, adequate procedures for reporting and accumulation of evidence.

**2** A ship to which this Annex applies may, in any port or offshore terminal of a Party, be subject to inspection by officers appointed or authorized by that Party for the purpose of verifying whether the ship has emitted any of the substances covered by this Annex in violation of the provision of this Annex. If an inspection indicates a violation of this Annex, a report shall be forwarded to the Administration for any appropriate action.

**3** Any Party shall furnish to the Administration evidence, if any, that the ship has emitted any of the substances covered by this Annex in violation of the provisions of this Annex. If it is practicable to do so, the competent authority of the former Party shall notify the master of the ship of the alleged violation.

**4** Upon receiving such evidence, the Administration so informed shall investigate the matter, and may request the other Party to furnish further or better evidence of the alleged contravention. If the Administration is satisfied that sufficient evidence is available to enable proceedings to be brought in respect of the alleged violation, it shall cause such proceedings to be taken in accordance with its law as soon as possible. The Administration shall promptly inform the Party that has reported the alleged violation, as well as the Organization, of the action taken.

**5** A Party may also inspect a ship to which this Annex applies when it enters the ports or offshore terminals under its jurisdiction, if a request for an investigation is received from any Party together with sufficient evidence that the ship has emitted any of the substances covered by the Annex in any place in violation of this Annex. The report of such investigation shall be sent to the Party requesting it and to the Administration so that the appropriate action may be taken under the present Convention.

**6** The international law concerning the prevention, reduction and control of pollution of the marine environment from ships, including that law relating to enforcement and safeguards, in force at the time of application or interpretation of this Annex, applies, *mutatis mutandis*, to the rules and standards set forth in this Annex.

# Chapter 3
## *Requirements for control of emissions from ships*

### Regulation 12
*Ozone-depleting substances*

**1** This regulation does not apply to permanently sealed equipment where there are no refrigerant charging connections or potentially removable components containing ozone-depleting substances.

**2** Subject to the provisions of regulation 3.1, any deliberate emissions of ozone-depleting substances shall be prohibited. Deliberate emissions include emissions occurring in the course of maintaining, servicing, repairing or disposing of systems or equipment, except that deliberate emissions do not include minimal releases associated with the recapture or recycling of an ozone-depleting substance. Emissions arising from leaks of an ozone-depleting substance, whether or not the leaks are deliberate, may be regulated by Parties.

**3.1** Installations that contain ozone-depleting substances, other than hydrochlorofluorocarbons, shall be prohibited:

- **.1** on ships constructed on or after 19 May 2005; or
- **.2** in the case of ships constructed before 19 May 2005, which have a contractual delivery date of the equipment to the ship on or after 19 May 2005 or, in the absence of a contractual delivery date, the actual delivery of the equipment to the ship on or after 19 May 2005.

**3.2** Installations that contain hydrochlorofluorocarbons shall be prohibited:

- **.1** on ships constructed on or after 1 January 2020; or
- **.2** in the case of ships constructed before 1 January 2020, which have a contractual delivery date of the equipment to the ship on or after 1 January 2020 or, in the absence of a contractual delivery date, the actual delivery of the equipment to the ship on or after 1 January 2020.

**4** The substances referred to in this regulation, and equipment containing such substances, shall be delivered to appropriate reception facilities when removed from ships.

**5** Each ship subject to regulation 6.1 shall maintain a list of equipment containing ozone-depleting substances.*

**6** Each ship subject to regulation 6.1 that has rechargeable systems that contain ozone-depleting substances shall maintain an *ozone-depleting substances record book*. This record book may form part of an existing logbook or electronic recording system as approved by the Administration.

**7** Entries in the ozone-depleting substances record book shall be recorded in terms of mass (kg) of substance and shall be completed without delay on each occasion, in respect of the following:

**.1** recharge, full or partial, of equipment containing ozone-depleting substances;

**.2** repair or maintenance of equipment containing ozone-depleting substances;

**.3** discharge of ozone-depleting substances to the atmosphere:

**.3.1** deliberate; and

**.3.2** non-deliberate;

**.4** discharge of ozone-depleting substances to land-based reception facilities; and

**.5** supply of ozone-depleting substances to the ship.

## Regulation 13

*Nitrogen oxides ($NO_x$)*

### Application

**1.1** This regulation shall apply to:

**.1** each marine diesel engine with a power output of more than 130 kW installed on a ship; and

**.2** each marine diesel engine with a power output of more than 130 kW that undergoes a major conversion on or after 1 January 2000 except when demonstrated to the satisfaction of the Administration that such engine is an identical replacement to the engine that it is replacing and is otherwise not covered under paragraph 1.1.1 of this regulation.

* See appendix I, Supplement to International Air Pollution Prevention Certificate (IAPP Certificate), section 2.1.

**1.2** This regulation does not apply to:

**.1** a marine diesel engine intended to be used solely for emergencies, or solely to power any device or equipment intended to be used solely for emergencies on the ship on which it is installed, or a marine diesel engine installed in lifeboats intended to be used solely for emergencies; and

**.2** a marine diesel engine installed on a ship solely engaged in voyages within waters subject to the sovereignty or jurisdiction of the State the flag of which the ship is entitled to fly, provided that such engine is subject to an alternative $NO_x$ control measure established by the Administration.

**1.3** Notwithstanding the provisions of paragraph 1.1 of this regulation, the Administration may provide an exclusion from the application of this regulation for any marine diesel engine that is installed on a ship constructed, or for any marine diesel engine that undergoes a major conversion, before 19 May 2005, provided that the ship on which the engine is installed is solely engaged in voyages to ports or offshore terminals within the State the flag of which the ship is entitled to fly.

### Major conversion

**2.1** For the purpose of this regulation, *major conversion* means a modification on or after 1 January 2000 of a marine diesel engine that has not already been certified to the standards set forth in paragraph 3, 4, or 5.1.1 of this regulation where:

**.1** the engine is replaced by a marine diesel engine or an additional marine diesel engine is installed, or

**.2** any substantial modification, as defined in the revised $NO_x$ Technical Code 2008, is made to the engine, or

**.3** the maximum continuous rating of the engine is increased by more than 10% compared to the maximum continuous rating of the original certification of the engine.

**2.2** For a major conversion involving the replacement of a marine diesel engine with a non-identical marine diesel engine or the installation of an additional marine diesel engine, the standards in this regulation in force at the time of the replacement or addition of the engine shall apply. On or after 1 January 2016, in the case of replacement engines only, if it is not possible for such a replacement engine to meet the standards set forth in paragraph 5.1.1 of this regulation (Tier III), then that replacement engine shall meet the standards set forth in paragraph 4 of this regulation (Tier II). Guidelines are to be developed by the Organization to set forth the criteria of when it is not possible for a replacement engine to meet the standards in paragraph 5.1.1 of this regulation.

**2.3** A marine diesel engine referred to in paragraph 2.1.2 or 2.1.3 of this regulation shall meet the following standards:

**.1** for ships constructed prior to 1 January 2000, the standards set forth in paragraph 3 of this regulation shall apply; and

**.2** for ships constructed on or after 1 January 2000, the standards in force at the time the ship was constructed shall apply.

### Tier I

**3** Subject to regulation 3 of this Annex, the operation of a marine diesel engine that is installed on a ship constructed on or after 1 January 2000 and prior to 1 January 2011 is prohibited, except when the emission of nitrogen oxides (calculated as the total weighted emission of $NO_2$) from the engine is within the following limits, where $n$ = rated engine speed (crankshaft revolutions per minute):

**.1** 17.0 g/kWh when $n$ is less than 130 rpm;

**.2** $45 \cdot n^{(-0.2)}$ g/kWh when $n$ is 130 or more but less than 2,000 rpm;

**.3** 9.8 g/kWh when $n$ is 2,000 rpm or more.

### Tier II

**4** Subject to regulation 3 of this Annex, the operation of a marine diesel engine that is installed on a ship constructed on or after 1 January 2011 is prohibited, except when the emission of nitrogen oxides (calculated as the total weighted emission of $NO_2$) from the engine is within the following limits, where $n$ = rated engine speed (crankshaft revolutions per minute):

**.1** 14.4 g/kWh when $n$ is less than 130 rpm;

**.2** $44 \cdot n^{(-0.23)}$ g/kWh when $n$ is 130 or more but less than 2,000 rpm;

**.3** 7.7 g/kWh when $n$ is 2,000 rpm or more.

## Tier III

**5.1** Subject to regulation 3 of this Annex, the operation of a marine diesel engine that is installed on a ship constructed on or after 1 January 2016:

- **.1** is prohibited except when the emission of nitrogen oxides (calculated as the total weighted emission of $NO_2$) from the engine is within the following limits, where $n$ = rated engine speed (crankshaft revolutions per minute):
  - **.1.1** 3.4 g/kWh when $n$ is less than 130 rpm;
  - **.1.2** $9 \cdot n^{(-0.2)}$ g/kWh when $n$ is 130 or more but less than 2,000 rpm; and
  - **.1.3** 2.0 g/kWh when $n$ is 2,000 rpm or more;
- **.2** is subject to the standards set forth in paragraph 5.1.1 of this regulation when the ship is operating in an emission control area designated under paragraph 6 of this regulation; and
- **.3** is subject to the standards set forth in paragraph 4 of this regulation when the ship is operating outside of an emission control area designated under paragraph 6 of this regulation.

**5.2** Subject to the review set forth in paragraph 10 of this regulation, the standards set forth in paragraph 5.1.1 of this regulation shall not apply to:

- **.1** a marine diesel engine installed on a ship with a length ($L$), as defined in regulation 1.19 of Annex I to the present Convention, less than 24 metres when it has been specifically designed, and is used solely, for recreational purposes; or
- **.2** a marine diesel engine installed on a ship with a combined nameplate diesel engine propulsion power of less than 750 kW if it is demonstrated, to the satisfaction of the Administration, that the ship cannot comply with the standards set forth in paragraph 5.1.1 of this regulation because of design or construction limitations of the ship.

## Emission control area

**6** For the purpose of this regulation, an emission control area shall be any sea area, including any port area, designated by the Organization in accordance with the criteria and procedures set forth in appendix III to this Annex.

## Marine diesel engines installed on a ship constructed prior to 1 January 2000

**7.1** Notwithstanding paragraph 1.1.1 of this regulation, a marine diesel engine with a power output of more than 5,000 kW and a per cylinder displacement at or above 90 litres installed on a ship constructed on or after 1 January 1990 but prior to 1 January 2000 shall comply with the emission limits set forth in paragraph 7.4 of this regulation, provided that an approved method for that engine has been certified by an Administration of a Party and notification of such certification has been submitted to the Organization by the certifying Administration. Compliance with this paragraph shall be demonstrated through one of the following:

- **.1** installation of the certified approved method, as confirmed by a survey using the verification procedure specified in the approved method file, including appropriate notation on the ship's International Air Pollution Prevention Certificate of the presence of the approved method; or
- **.2** certification of the engine confirming that it operates within the limits set forth in paragraph 3, 4, or 5.1.1 of this regulation and an appropriate notation of the engine certification on the ship's International Air Pollution Prevention Certificate.

**7.2** Paragraph 7.1 of this regulation shall apply no later than the first renewal survey that occurs 12 months or more after deposit of the notification in paragraph 7.1. If a shipowner of a ship on which an approved method is to be installed can demonstrate to the satisfaction of the Administration that the approved method was not commercially available despite best efforts to obtain it, then that approved method shall be installed on the ship no later than the next annual survey of that ship that falls after the approved method is commercially available.

**7.3** With regard to a ship with a marine diesel engine with a power output of more than 5,000 kW and a per cylinder displacement at or above 90 litres installed on a ship constructed on or after 1 January 1990 but prior to 1 January 2000, the International Air Pollution Prevention Certificate shall, for a marine diesel engine to which paragraph 7.1 of this regulation applies, indicate that either an approved method has been applied pursuant to paragraph 7.1.1 of this regulation or the engine has been certified pursuant to paragraph 7.1.2 of this regulation or that an approved method does not yet exist or is not yet commercially available as described in paragraph 7.2 of this regulation.

**7.4** Subject to regulation 3 of this Annex, the operation of a marine diesel engine described in paragraph 7.1 of this regulation is prohibited, except when the emission of nitrogen oxides (calculated as the total weighted emission of $NO_2$) from the engine is within the following limits, where $n$ = rated engine speed (crankshaft revolutions per minute):

**.1** 17.0 g/kWh when $n$ is less than 130 rpm;

**.2** $45 \cdot n^{(-0.2)}$ g/kWh when $n$ is 130 or more but less than 2,000 rpm; and

**.3** 9.8 g/kWh when $n$ is 2,000 rpm or more.

**7.5** Certification of an approved method shall be in accordance with chapter 7 of the revised $NO_x$ Technical Code 2008 and shall include verification:

**.1** by the designer of the base marine diesel engine to which the approved method applies that the calculated effect of the approved method will not decrease engine rating by more than 1.0%, increase fuel consumption by more than 2.0% as measured according to the appropriate test cycle set forth in the revised $NO_x$ Technical Code 2008, or adversely affect engine durability or reliability; and

**.2** that the cost of the approved method is not excessive, which is determined by a comparison of the amount of $NO_x$ reduced by the approved method to achieve the standard set forth in paragraph 7.4 of this regulation and the cost of purchasing and installing such approved method.*

* The cost of an approved method shall not exceed 375 Special Drawing Rights/metric tonne $NO_x$ calculated in accordance with the cost-effectiveness (Ce) formula below:

$$Ce = \frac{\text{Cost of approved method} \cdot 10^6}{\text{Power(kW)} \cdot 0.768 \cdot 6{,}000\text{(hours/year)} \cdot 5\text{(years)} \cdot \Delta NO_x\text{(g/kWh)}}$$

### Certification

**8** The revised $NO_x$ Technical Code 2008 shall be applied in the certification, testing and measurement procedures for the standards set forth in this regulation.

**9** The procedures for determining $NO_x$ emissions set out in the revised $NO_x$ Technical Code 2008 are intended to be representative of the normal operation of the engine. Defeat devices and irrational emission control strategies undermine this intention and shall not be allowed. This regulation shall not prevent the use of auxiliary control devices that are used to protect the engine and/or its ancillary equipment against operating conditions that could result in damage or failure or that are used to facilitate the starting of the engine.

### Review

**10** Beginning in 2012 and completed no later than 2013, the Organization shall review the status of the technological developments to implement the standards set forth in paragraph 5.1.1 of this regulation and shall, if proven necessary, adjust the time periods (effective date) set forth in that paragraph.

## Regulation 14

*Sulphur oxides ($SO_x$) and particulate matter*

### General requirements

**1** The sulphur content of any fuel oil used on board ships shall not exceed the following limits:

- **.1** 4.50% m/m prior to 1 January 2012;
- **.2** 3.50% m/m on and after 1 January 2012; and
- **.3** 0.50% m/m on and after 1 January 2020.

**2** The worldwide average sulphur content of residual fuel oil supplied for use on board ships shall be monitored taking into account guidelines developed by the Organization.*

* MEPC.82(43), Guidelines for monitoring the world-wide average sulphur content of residual fuel oils supplied for use on board ships.

**Requirements within emission control areas**

**3** For the purpose of this regulation, emission control areas shall include:

**.1** the Baltic Sea area as defined in regulation 1.11.2 of Annex I, the North Sea as defined in regulation 5(1)(f) of Annex V; and

**.2** any other sea area, including port areas, designated by the Organization in accordance with criteria and procedures set forth in appendix III to this Annex.

**4** While ships are operating within an emission control area, the sulphur content of fuel oil used on board ships shall not exceed the following limits:

**.1** 1.50% m/m prior to 1 July 2010;

**.2** 1.00% m/m on and after 1 July 2010; and

**.3** 0.10% m/m on and after 1 January 2015.

**5** The sulphur content of fuel oil referred to in paragraph 1 and paragraph 4 of this regulation shall be documented by its supplier as required by regulation 18 of this Annex.

**6** Those ships using separate fuel oils to comply with paragraph 4 of this regulation and entering or leaving an emission control area set forth in paragraph 3 of this regulation shall carry a written procedure showing how the fuel oil changeover is to be done, allowing sufficient time for the fuel oil service system to be fully flushed of all fuel oils exceeding the applicable sulphur content specified in paragraph 4 of this regulation prior to entry into an emission control area. The volume of low sulphur fuel oils in each tank as well as the date, time and position of the ship when any fuel oil changeover operation is completed prior to the entry into an emission control area or commenced after exit from such an area shall be recorded in such logbook as prescribed by the Administration.

**7** During the first twelve months immediately following an amendment designating a specific emission control area under paragraph 3.2 of this regulation, ships operating in that emission control area are exempt from the requirements in paragraphs 4 and 6 of this regulation and from the requirements of paragraph 5 of this regulation insofar as they relate to paragraph 4 of this regulation.

### Review provision

**8** A review of the standard set forth in paragraph 1.3 of this regulation shall be completed by 2018 to determine the availability of fuel oil to comply with the fuel oil standard set forth in that paragraph and shall take into account the following elements:

**.1** the global market supply and demand for fuel oil to comply with paragraph 1.3 of this regulation that exist at the time that the review is conducted;

**.2** an analysis of the trends in fuel oil markets; and

**.3** any other relevant issue.

**9** The Organization shall establish a group of experts, comprising representatives with the appropriate expertise in the fuel oil market and appropriate maritime, environmental, scientific and legal expertise, to conduct the review referred to in paragraph 8 of this regulation. The group of experts shall develop the appropriate information to inform the decision to be taken by the Parties.

**10** The Parties, based on the information developed by the group of experts, may decide whether it is possible for ships to comply with the date in paragraph 1.3 of this regulation. If a decision is taken that it is not possible for ships to comply, then the standard in that paragraph shall become effective on 1 January 2025.

## Regulation 15

*Volatile organic compounds (VOCs)*

**1** If the emissions of VOCs from a tanker are to be regulated in a port or ports or a terminal or terminals under the jurisdiction of a Party, they shall be regulated in accordance with the provisions of this regulation.

**2** A Party regulating tankers for VOC emissions shall submit a notification to the Organization. This notification shall include information on the size of tankers to be controlled, the cargoes requiring vapour emission control systems and the effective date of such control. The notification shall be submitted at least six months before the effective date.

**3** A Party that designates ports or terminals at which VOC emissions from tankers are to be regulated shall ensure that vapour emission control systems, approved by that Party taking into account the safety standards for such systems developed by the Organization*, are provided in any designated port and terminal and are operated safely and in a manner so as to avoid undue delay to a ship.

**4** The Organization shall circulate a list of the ports and terminals designated by Parties to other Parties and Member States of the Organization for their information.

**5** A tanker to which paragraph 1 of this regulation applies shall be provided with a vapour emission collection system approved by the Administration taking into account the safety standards for such systems developed by the Organization*, and shall use this system during the loading of relevant cargoes. A port or terminal that has installed vapour emission control systems in accordance with this regulation may accept tankers that are not fitted with vapour collection systems for a period of three years after the effective date identified in paragraph 2 of this regulation.

**6** A tanker carrying crude oil shall have on board and implement a VOC management plan approved by the Administration. Such a plan shall be prepared taking into account the guidelines developed by the Organization. The plan shall be specific to each ship and shall at least:

- **.1** provide written procedures for minimizing VOC emissions during the loading, sea passage and discharge of cargo;
- **.2** give consideration to the additional VOC generated by crude oil washing;
- **.3** identify a person responsible for implementing the plan; and
- **.4** for ships on international voyages, be written in the working language of the master and officers and, if the working language of the master and officers is not English, French or Spanish, include a translation into one of these languages.

**7** This regulation shall also apply to gas carriers only if the types of loading and containment systems allow safe retention of non-methane VOCs on board or their safe return ashore.†

---

* MSC/Circ.585, Standards for vapour emission control systems.

† MSC.30(61), International Code for the Construction and Equipment of Ships Carrying Liquefied Gases in Bulk.

## Regulation 16

*Shipboard incineration*

**1** Except as provided in paragraph 4 of this regulation, shipboard incineration shall be allowed only in a shipboard incinerator.

**2** Shipboard incineration of the following substances shall be prohibited:

- **.1** residues of cargoes subject to Annex I, II or III or related contaminated packing materials;
- **.2** polychlorinated biphenyls (PCBs);
- **.3** garbage, as defined by Annex V, containing more than traces of heavy metals;
- **.4** refined petroleum products containing halogen compounds;
- **.5** sewage sludge and sludge oil either of which is not generated on board the ship; and
- **.6** exhaust gas cleaning system residues.

**3** Shipboard incineration of polyvinyl chlorides (PVCs) shall be prohibited, except in shipboard incinerators for which IMO Type Approval Certificates* have been issued.

**4** Shipboard incineration of sewage sludge and sludge oil generated during normal operation of a ship may also take place in the main or auxiliary power plant or boilers, but in those cases, shall not take place inside ports, harbours and estuaries.

**5** Nothing in this regulation neither:

- **.1** affects the prohibition in, or other requirements of, the Convention on the Prevention of Marine Pollution by Dumping of Wastes and Other Matter, 1972, as amended, and the 1996 Protocol thereto, nor
- **.2** precludes the development, installation and operation of alternative design shipboard thermal waste treatment devices that meet or exceed the requirements of this regulation.

**6.1** Except as provided in paragraph 6.2 of this regulation, each incinerator on a ship constructed on or after 1 January 2000 or incinerator that is installed on board a ship on or after 1 January 2000 shall meet the requirements contained in appendix IV to this Annex.

---

* Type Approval Certificates issued in accordance with resolution MEPC.59(33), Revised guidelines for the implementation of Annex V of MARPOL 73/78, or MEPC.76(40), Standard specification for shipboard incinerators.

Each incinerator subject to this paragraph shall be approved by the Administration taking into account the standard specification for shipboard incinerators developed by the Organization*; or

**6.2** The Administration may allow exclusion from the application of paragraph 6.1 of this regulation to any incinerator installed on board a ship before 19 May 2005, provided that the ship is solely engaged in voyages within waters subject to the sovereignty or jurisdiction of the State the flag of which the ship is entitled to fly.

**7** Incinerators installed in accordance with the requirements of paragraph 6.1 of this regulation shall be provided with a manufacturer's operating manual, which is to be retained with the unit and which shall specify how to operate the incinerator within the limits described in paragraph 2 of appendix IV of this Annex.

**8** Personnel responsible for the operation of an incinerator installed in accordance with the requirements of paragraph 6.1 of this regulation shall be trained to implement the guidance provided in the manufacturer's operating manual as required by paragraph 7 of this regulation.

**9** For incinerators installed in accordance with the requirements of paragraph 6.1 of this regulation the combustion chamber gas outlet temperature shall be monitored at all times the unit is in operation. Where that incinerator is of the continuous-feed type, waste shall not be fed into the unit when the combustion chamber gas outlet temperature is below 850°C. Where that incinerator is of the batch-loaded type, the unit shall be designed so that the combustion chamber gas outlet temperature shall reach 600°C within five minutes after start-up and will thereafter stabilize at a temperature not less than 850°C.

## Regulation 17
*Reception facilities*

**1** Each Party undertakes to ensure the provision of facilities adequate to meet the:

- **.1** needs of ships using its repair ports for the reception of ozone-depleting substances and equipment containing such substances when removed from ships;

* Refer to resolution MEPC.76(40), as modified by resolution MEPC.93(45), Standard specification for shipboard incinerators.

**.2** needs of ships using its ports, terminals or repair ports for the reception of exhaust gas cleaning residues from an exhaust gas cleaning system;

without causing undue delay to ships, and

**.3** needs in ship-breaking facilities for the reception of ozone-depleting substances and equipment containing such substances when removed from ships.

**2** If a particular port or terminal of a Party is – taking into account the guidelines to be developed by the Organization – remotely located from, or lacking in, the industrial infrastructure necessary to manage and process those substances referred to in paragraph 1 of this regulation and therefore cannot accept such substances, then the Party shall inform the Organization of any such port or terminal so that this information may be circulated to all Parties and Member States of the Organization for their information and any appropriate action. Each Party that has provided the Organization with such information shall also notify the Organization of its ports and terminals where reception facilities are available to manage and process such substances.

**3** Each Party shall notify the Organization for transmission to the Members of the Organization of all cases where the facilities provided under this regulation are unavailable or alleged to be inadequate.

## Regulation 18

*Fuel oil availability and quality*

### Fuel oil availability

**1** Each Party shall take all reasonable steps to promote the availability of fuel oils that comply with this Annex and inform the Organization of the availability of compliant fuel oils in its ports and terminals.

**2.1** If a ship is found by a Party not to be in compliance with the standards for compliant fuel oils set forth in this Annex, the competent authority of the Party is entitled to require the ship to:

**.1** present a record of the actions taken to attempt to achieve compliance; and

**.2** provide evidence that it attempted to purchase compliant fuel oil in accordance with its voyage plan and, if it was not made available where planned, that attempts were made to locate alternative sources for such fuel oil and that despite best efforts to obtain compliant fuel oil, no such fuel oil was made available for purchase.

**2.2** The ship should not be required to deviate from its intended voyage or to delay unduly the voyage in order to achieve compliance.

**2.3** If a ship provides the information set forth in paragraph 2.1 of this regulation, a Party shall take into account all relevant circumstances and the evidence presented to determine the appropriate action to take, including not taking control measures.

**2.4** A ship shall notify its Administration and the competent authority of the relevant port of destination when it cannot purchase compliant fuel oil.

**2.5** A Party shall notify the Organization when a ship has presented evidence of the non-availability of compliant fuel oil.

## Fuel oil quality

**3** Fuel oil for combustion purposes delivered to and used on board ships to which this Annex applies shall meet the following requirements:

**.1** except as provided in paragraph 3.2 of this regulation:

**.1.1** the fuel oil shall be blends of hydrocarbons derived from petroleum refining. This shall not preclude the incorporation of small amounts of additives intended to improve some aspects of performance;

**.1.2** the fuel oil shall be free from inorganic acid; and

**.1.3** the fuel oil shall not include any added substance or chemical waste that:

**.1.3.1** jeopardizes the safety of ships or adversely affects the performance of the machinery, or

**.1.3.2** is harmful to personnel, or

**.1.3.3** contributes overall to additional air pollution.

**.2** fuel oil for combustion purposes derived by methods other than petroleum refining shall not:

**.2.1** exceed the applicable sulphur content set forth in regulation 14 of this Annex;

**.2.2** cause an engine to exceed the applicable $NO_x$ emission limit set forth in paragraphs 3, 4, 5.1.1 and 7.4 of regulation 13;

**.2.3** contain inorganic acid; or

**.2.4.1** jeopardize the safety of ships or adversely affect the performance of the machinery, or

**.2.4.2** be harmful to personnel, or

**.2.4.3** contribute overall to additional air pollution.

**4** This regulation does not apply to coal in its solid form or nuclear fuels. Paragraphs 5, 6, 7.1, 7.2, 8.1, 8.2, 9.2, 9.3, and 9.4 of this regulation do not apply to gas fuels such as liquified natural gas, compressed natural gas or liquified petroleum gas. The sulphur content of gas fuels delivered to a ship specifically for combustion purposes on board that ship shall be documented by the supplier.

**5** For each ship subject to regulations 5 and 6 of this Annex, details of fuel oil for combustion purposes delivered to and used on board shall be recorded by means of a bunker delivery note that shall contain at least the information specified in appendix V to this Annex.

**6** The bunker delivery note shall be kept on board the ship in such a place as to be readily available for inspection at all reasonable times. It shall be retained for a period of three years after the fuel oil has been delivered on board.

**7.1** The competent authority of a Party may inspect the bunker delivery notes on board any ship to which this Annex applies while the ship is in its port or offshore terminal, may make a copy of each delivery note, and may require the master or person in charge of the ship to certify that each copy is a true copy of such bunker delivery note. The competent authority may also verify the contents of each note through consultations with the port where the note was issued.

**7.2** The inspection of the bunker delivery notes and the taking of certified copies by the competent authority under this paragraph shall be performed as expeditiously as possible without causing the ship to be unduly delayed.

**8.1** The bunker delivery note shall be accompanied by a representative sample of the fuel oil delivered taking into account guidelines developed by the Organization.* The sample is to be sealed and signed by the supplier's representative and the master or officer in charge of the bunker operation on completion of bunkering operations and retained under the ship's control until the fuel oil is substantially consumed, but in any case for a period of not less than 12 months from the time of delivery.

**8.2** If an Administration requires the representative sample to be analysed, it shall be done in accordance with the verification procedure set forth in appendix VI to determine whether the fuel oil meets the requirements of this Annex.

**9** Parties undertake to ensure that appropriate authorities designated by them:

**.1** maintain a register of local suppliers of fuel oil;

**.2** require local suppliers to provide the bunker delivery note and sample as required by this regulation, certified by the fuel oil supplier that the fuel oil meets the requirements of regulations 14 and 18 of this Annex;

**.3** require local suppliers to retain a copy of the bunker delivery note for at least three years for inspection and verification by the port State as necessary;

**.4** take action as appropriate against fuel oil suppliers that have been found to deliver fuel oil that does not comply with that stated on the bunker delivery note;

**.5** inform the Administration of any ship receiving fuel oil found to be non-compliant with the requirements of regulation 14 or 18 of this Annex; and

**.6** inform the Organization for transmission to Parties and Member States of the Organization of all cases where fuel oil suppliers have failed to meet the requirements specified in regulations 14 or 18 of this Annex.

---

* Refer to MEPC.96(47), Guidelines for the sampling of fuel oil for determination of compliance with Annex VI of MARPOL 73/78.

**10** In connection with port State inspections carried out by Parties, the Parties further undertake to:

- **.1** inform the Party or non-Party under whose jurisdiction a bunker delivery note was issued of cases of delivery of non-compliant fuel oil, giving all relevant information; and
- **.2** ensure that remedial action as appropriate is taken to bring non-compliant fuel oil discovered into compliance.

**11** For every ship of 400 gross tonnage and above on scheduled services with frequent and regular port calls, an Administration may decide after application and consultation with affected States that compliance with paragraph 6 of this regulation may be documented in an alternative manner that gives similar certainty of compliance with regulations 14 and 18 of this Annex.

# *Appendix I*

## Form of International Air Pollution Prevention (IAPP) Certificate (Regulation 8)

### INTERNATIONAL AIR POLLUTION PREVENTION CERTIFICATE

Issued under the provisions of the Protocol of 1997, as amended by resolution MEPC.176(58) in 2008, to amend the International Convention for the Prevention of Pollution from Ships, 1973, as modified by the Protocol of 1978 related thereto (hereinafter referred to as "the Convention") under the authority of the Government of:

. . . . . . . . . . . . . . . . . . . . . . . . . . . . . . . . . . . . . . . . . . . . . .

*(Full designation of the country)*

by. . . . . . . . . . . . . . . . . . . . . . . . . . . . . . . . . . . . . . . . . . . . .

*(Full designation of the competent person or organization authorized under the provisions of the Convention)*

**Particulars of ship***

Name of ship . . . . . . . . . . . . . . . . . . . . . . . . . . . . . . . . . . . .

Distinctive number or letters . . . . . . . . . . . . . . . . . . . . . . . . . .

Port of registry . . . . . . . . . . . . . . . . . . . . . . . . . . . . . . . . . . .

Gross tonnage . . . . . . . . . . . . . . . . . . . . . . . . . . . . . . . . . . .

IMO Number† . . . . . . . . . . . . . . . . . . . . . . . . . . . . . . . . . . . .

* Alternatively, the particulars of the ship may be placed horizontally in boxes.

† In accordance with the IMO ship identification number scheme, adopted by the Organization by resolution A.600(15).

THIS IS TO CERTIFY:

1 That the ship has been surveyed in accordance with regulation 5 of Annex VI of the Convention; and

2 That the survey shows that the equipment, systems, fittings, arrangements and materials fully comply with the applicable requirements of Annex VI of the Convention.

Completion date of survey on which this Certificate is based:

. . . . . . . . . . . . . . . . . . . . . . . . . . . . . . . . . . . . . (dd/mm/yyyy)

This Certificate is valid until . . . . . . . . . . . . . . . . . . . . . . . * subject to surveys in accordance with regulation 5 of Annex VI of the Convention.

Issued at . . . . . . . . . . . . . . . . . . . . . . . . . . . . . . . . . . . . . . .
*(Place of issue of certificate)*

(dd/mm/yyyy): . . . . . . . . . . . . . . . . . . . . . . . . . . . . . . . . . . . . . . . . .
*(Date of issue)* *(Signature of authorized official issuing the certificate)*

*(Seal or stamp of the authority, as appropriate)*

* Insert the date of expiry as specified by the Administration in accordance with regulation 9.1 of Annex VI of the Convention. The day and the month of this date correspond to the anniversary date as defined in regulation 2.3 of Annex VI of the Convention, unless amended in accordance with regulation 9.8 of Annex VI of the Convention.

**Endorsement for annual and intermediate surveys**

THIS IS TO CERTIFY that at a survey required by regulation 5 of Annex VI of the Convention the ship was found to comply with the relevant provisions of that Annex:

Annual survey: Signed:. . . . . . . . . . . . . . . . . . . . . .

*(Signature of authorized official)*

Place:. . . . . . . . . . . . . . . . . . . . . . .

Date (dd/mm/yyyy): . . . . . . . . . . . .

*(Seal or stamp of the authority, as appropriate)*

Annual/Intermediate* survey: Signed: . . . . . . . . . . . . . . . . . . . . . .

*(Signature of authorized official)*

Place:. . . . . . . . . . . . . . . . . . . . . . .

Date (dd/mm/yyyy): . . . . . . . . . . . .

*(Seal or stamp of the authority, as appropriate)*

Annual/Intermediate* survey: Signed: . . . . . . . . . . . . . . . . . . . . . .

*(Signature of authorized official)*

Place:. . . . . . . . . . . . . . . . . . . . . . .

Date (dd/mm/yyyy): . . . . . . . . . . . .

*(Seal or stamp of the authority, as appropriate)*

Annual survey: Signed:. . . . . . . . . . . . . . . . . . . . . .

*(Signature of authorized official)*

Place:. . . . . . . . . . . . . . . . . . . . . . .

Date (dd/mm/yyyy): . . . . . . . . . . . .

*(Seal or stamp of the authority, as appropriate)*

* Delete as appropriate.

**Annual/intermediate survey in accordance with regulation 9.8.3**

THIS IS TO CERTIFY that, at an annual/intermediate* survey in accordance with regulation 9.8.3 of Annex VI of the Convention, the ship was found to comply with the relevant provisions of that Annex:

Signed:. . . . . . . . . . . . . . . . . . . . .

*(Signature of authorized official)*

Place: . . . . . . . . . . . . . . . . . . . . . .

Date (dd/mm/yyyy): . . . . . . . . . . .

*(Seal or stamp of the authority, as appropriate)*

**Endorsement to extend the certificate if valid for less than 5 years where regulation 9.3 applies**

The ship complies with the relevant provisions of the Annex, and this certificate shall, in accordance with regulation 9.3 of Annex VI of the Convention, be accepted as valid until (dd/mm/yyyy): . . . .

Signed:. . . . . . . . . . . . . . . . . . . . .

*(Signature of authorized official)*

Place: . . . . . . . . . . . . . . . . . . . . . .

Date (dd/mm/yyyy): . . . . . . . . . . .

*(Seal or stamp of the authority, as appropriate)*

**Endorsement where the renewal survey has been completed and regulation 9.4 applies**

The ship complies with the relevant provisions of the Annex, and this certificate shall, in accordance with regulation 9.4 of Annex VI of the Convention, be accepted as valid until (dd/mm/yyyy): . . . .

Signed:. . . . . . . . . . . . . . . . . . . . .

*(Signature of authorized official)*

Place: . . . . . . . . . . . . . . . . . . . . . .

Date (dd/mm/yyyy): . . . . . . . . . . .

*(Seal or stamp of the authority, as appropriate)*

* Delete as appropriate.

**Endorsement to extend the validity of the certificate until reaching the port of survey or for a period of grace where regulation 9.5 or 9.6 applies**

This certificate shall, in accordance with regulation 9.5 or 9.6* of Annex VI of the Convention, be accepted as valid until (dd/mm/yyyy): . . . . . . . . . . . . . . . . . . . . . . . . . . . . . . . . . . . . . . . .

Signed:. . . . . . . . . . . . . . . . . . . . . . .

*(Signature of authorized official)*

Place:. . . . . . . . . . . . . . . . . . . . . . . . .

Date (dd/mm/yyyy): . . . . . . . . . . . . .

*(Seal or stamp of the authority, as appropriate)*

**Endorsement for advancement of anniversary date where regulation 9.8 applies**

In accordance with regulation 9.8 of Annex VI of the Convention, the new anniversary date is (dd/mm/yyyy): . . . . . . . . . . . . . . . . . . . .

Signed:. . . . . . . . . . . . . . . . . . . . . . .

*(Signature of authorized official)*

Place:. . . . . . . . . . . . . . . . . . . . . . . . .

Date (dd/mm/yyyy): . . . . . . . . . . . . .

*(Seal or stamp of the authority, as appropriate)*

In accordance with regulation 9.8 of Annex VI of the Convention, the new anniversary date is (dd/mm/yyyy): . . . . . . . . . . . . . . . . . . . .

Signed:. . . . . . . . . . . . . . . . . . . . . . .

*(Signature of authorized official)*

Place:. . . . . . . . . . . . . . . . . . . . . . . . .

Date (dd/mm/yyyy): . . . . . . . . . . . . .

*(Seal or stamp of the authority, as appropriate)*

* Delete as appropriate.

## SUPPLEMENT TO INTERNATIONAL AIR POLLUTION PREVENTION CERTIFICATE (IAPP CERTIFICATE)

### RECORD OF CONSTRUCTION AND EQUIPMENT

*Notes:*

1 This Record shall be permanently attached to the IAPP Certificate. The IAPP Certificate shall be available on board the ship at all times.

2 The Record shall be at least in English, French or Spanish. If an official language of the issuing country is also used, this shall prevail in case of a dispute or discrepancy.

3 Entries in boxes shall be made by inserting either a cross (x) for the answer "yes" and "applicable" or a (–) for the answers "no" and "not applicable" as appropriate.

4 Unless otherwise stated, regulations mentioned in this Record refer to regulations of Annex VI of the Convention and resolutions or circulars refer to those adopted by the International Maritime Organization.

**1 Particulars of ship**

1.1 Name of ship. . . . . . . . . . . . . . . . . . . . . . . . . . . . . .

1.2 IMO Number.. . . . . . . . . . . . . . . . . . . . . . . . . . . . .

1.3 Date on which keel was laid or ship was at a similar stage of construction. . . . . . . . . . . . . . . . . . . . . . . . . . . . . . . . . . . .

1.4 Length (*L*)* metres . . . . . . . . . . . . . . . . . . . . . . . . . . .

**2 Control of emissions from ships**

2.1 *Ozone-depleting substances (regulation 12)*

2.1.1 The following fire-extinguishing systems, other systems and equipment containing ozone-depleting substances, other than

* Completed only in respect of ships constructed on or after 1 January 2016 that are specially designed, and used solely, for recreational purposes and to which, in accordance with regulation 13.5.2.1, the $NO_x$ emission limit as given by regulation 13.5.1.1 will not apply.

hydrochlorofluorocarbons (HCFCs), installed before 19 May 2005 may continue in service:

| System or equipment | Location on board | Substance |
|---|---|---|
| | | |

2.1.2 The following systems containing HCFCs installed before 1 January 2020 may continue in service:

| System or equipment | Location on board | Substance |
|---|---|---|
| | | |

2.2 *Nitrogen oxides ($NO_x$) (regulation 13)*

2.2.1 The following marine diesel engines installed on this ship comply with the applicable emission limit of regulation 13 in accordance with the revised $NO_x$ Technical Code 2008:

| | | Engine #1 | Engine #2 | Engine #3 | Engine #4 | Engine #5 | Engine #6 |
|---|---|---|---|---|---|---|---|
| **Manufacturer and model** | | | | | | | |
| **Serial number** | | | | | | | |
| **Use** | | | | | | | |
| **Power output (kW)** | | | | | | | |
| **Rated speed (rpm)** | | | | | | | |
| **Date of installation (dd/mm/yyyy)** | | | | | | | |
| **Date of major conversion (dd/mm/yyyy)** | According to Reg. 13.2.2 | | | | | | |
| | According to Reg. 13.2.3 | | | | | | |

| **Exempted by regulation 13.1.1.2** | ☐ | ☐ | ☐ | ☐ | ☐ | ☐ |
|---|---|---|---|---|---|---|
| **Tier I** Reg.13.3 | ☐ | ☐ | ☐ | ☐ | ☐ | ☐ |
| **Tier II** Reg.13.4 | ☐ | ☐ | ☐ | ☐ | ☐ | ☐ |
| **Tier II** Reg. 13.2.2 or 13.5.2 | ☐ | ☐ | ☐ | ☐ | ☐ | ☐ |
| **Tier III** Reg.13.5.1.1 | ☐ | ☐ | ☐ | ☐ | ☐ | ☐ |
| **Approved method exists** | ☐ | ☐ | ☐ | ☐ | ☐ | ☐ |
| **Approved method not commercially available** | ☐ | ☐ | ☐ | ☐ | ☐ | ☐ |
| **Approved method installed** | ☐ | ☐ | ☐ | ☐ | ☐ | ☐ |

2.3 *Sulphur oxides ($SO_x$) and particulate matter (regulation 14)*

2.3.1 When the ship operates within an emission control area specified in regulation 14.3, the ship uses:

.1 fuel oil with a sulphur content that does not exceed the applicable limit value as documented by bunker delivery notes; or . . . . . . . . . . . . . . . . . . . . . . . . . . . . . . . . . . . . . ☐

.2 an equivalent arrangement approved in accordance with regulation 4.1 as listed in 2.6 . . . . . . . . . . . . . . . . . . . . ☐

2.4 *Volatile organic compounds (VOCs) (regulation 15)*

2.4.1 The tanker has a vapour collection system installed and approved in accordance with MSC/Circ.585. . . . . . . . . . . . . . . . ☐

2.4.2.1 For a tanker carrying crude oil, there is an approved VOC management plan . . . . . . . . . . . . . . . . . . . . . . . . . . . . . . . . . ☐

2.4.2.2 VOC management plan approval reference: . . . . . . . . . . .

2.5 *Shipboard incineration (regulation 16)*

The ship has an incinerator:

.1 installed on or after 1 January 2000 that complies with resolution MEPC.76(40) as amended . . . . . . . . . . . . . . ☐

.2 installed before 1 January 2000 that complies with:

.2.1 resolution MEPC.59(33). . . . . . . . . . . . . . . . . . . . ☐

.2.2 resolution MEPC.76(40). . . . . . . . . . . . . . . . . . . . ☐

2.6 *Equivalents (regulation 4)*

The ship has been allowed to use the following fitting, material, appliance or apparatus to be fitted in a ship or other procedures, alternative fuel oils, or compliance methods used as an alternative to that required by this Annex:

| System or equipment | Equivalent used | Approval reference |
|---|---|---|
| | | |

THIS IS TO CERTIFY that this Record is correct in all respects.

Issued at . . . . . . . . . . . . . . . . . . . . . . . . . . . . . . . . . . . . . . . .

*(Place of issue of the Record)*

(dd/mm/yyyy): . . . . . . . . . . . . . . . . . . . . . . . . . . . . . . . . . . . . . . .

*(Date of issue)* *(Signature of duly authorized official issuing the Record)*

*(Seal or stamp of the authority, as appropriate)*

# Appendix II

## Test cycles and weighting factors (Regulation 13)

The following test cycles and weighting factors shall be applied for verification of compliance of marine diesel engines with the applicable $NO_x$ limit in accordance with regulation 13 of this Annex using the test procedure and calculation method as specified in the revised $NO_x$ Technical Code 2008.

**.1** For constant-speed marine engines for ship main propulsion, including diesel-electric drive, test cycle E2 shall be applied;

**.2** For controllable-pitch propeller sets test cycle E2 shall be applied;

**.3** For propeller-law-operated main and propeller-law-operated auxiliary engines the test cycle E3 shall be applied;

**.4** For constant-speed auxiliary engines test cycle D2 shall be applied; and

**.5** For variable-speed, variable-load auxiliary engines, not included above, test cycle C1 shall be applied.

Test cycle for *constant-speed main propulsion* application (including diesel-electric drive and all controllable-pitch propeller installations)

| Test cycle type E2 | Speed | 100% | 100% | 100% | 100% |
|---|---|---|---|---|---|
| | Power | 100% | 75% | 50% | 25% |
| | Weighting factor | 0.2 | 0.5 | 0.15 | 0.15 |

Test cycle for *propeller-law-operated main* and *propeller-law-operated auxiliary engine* application

| Test cycle type E3 | Speed | 100% | 91% | 80% | 63% |
|---|---|---|---|---|---|
| | Power | 100% | 75% | 50% | 25% |
| | Weighting factor | 0.2 | 0.5 | 0.15 | 0.15 |

Test cycle for *constant-speed auxiliary engine* application

| | | | | | | |
|---|---|---|---|---|---|---|
| Test cycle type D2 | Speed | 100% | 100% | 100% | 100% | 100% |
| | Power | 100% | 75% | 50% | 25% | 10% |
| | Weighting factor | 0.05 | 0.25 | 0.3 | 0.3 | 0.1 |

Test cycle for *variable-speed and -load auxiliary engine* application

| | | | | | | | | | |
|---|---|---|---|---|---|---|---|---|---|
| Test cycle type C1 | Speed | Rated | | | | Intermediate | | | Idle |
| | Torque | 100% | 75% | 50% | 10% | 100% | 75% | 50% | 0% |
| | Weighting factor | 0.15 | 0.15 | 0.15 | 0.1 | 0.1 | 0.1 | 0.1 | 0.15 |

In the case of an engine to be certified in accordance with paragraph 5.1.1 of regulation 13, the specific emission at each individual mode point shall not exceed the applicable $NO_x$ emission limit value by more than 50% except as follows:

**.1** The 10% mode point in the D2 test cycle.

**.2** The 10% mode point in the C1 test cycle.

**.3** The idle mode point in the C1 test cycle.

# *Appendix III*

## Criteria and procedures for designation of emission control areas (Regulation 13.6 and regulation 14.3)

**1** *Objectives*

**1.1** The purpose of this appendix is to provide the criteria and procedures to Parties for the formulation and submission of proposals for the designation of emission control areas and to set forth the factors to be considered in the assessment of such proposals by the Organization.

**1.2** Emissions of $NO_x$, $SO_x$ and particulate matter from ocean-going ships contribute to ambient concentrations of air pollution in cities and coastal areas around the world. Adverse public health and environmental effects associated with air pollution include premature mortality, cardiopulmonary disease, lung cancer, chronic respiratory ailments, acidification and eutrophication.

**1.3** An emission control area should be considered for adoption by the Organization if supported by a demonstrated need to prevent, reduce and control emissions of $NO_x$ or $SO_x$ and particulate matter or all three types of emissions (hereinafter emissions) from ships.

**2** *Process for the designation of emission control areas*

**2.1** A proposal to the Organization for designation of an emission control area for $NO_x$ or $SO_x$ and particulate matter or all three types of emissions may be submitted only by Parties. Where two or more Parties have a common interest in a particular area, they should formulate a coordinated proposal.

**2.2** A proposal to designate a given area as an emission control area should be submitted to the Organization in accordance with the rules and procedures established by the Organization.

**3** *Criteria for designation of an emission control area*

**3.1** The proposal shall include:

**.1** a clear delineation of the proposed area of application, along with a reference chart on which the area is marked;

**.2** the type or types of emission(s) that is or are being proposed for control (i.e., $NO_x$ or $SO_x$ and particulate matter or all three types of emissions);

**.3** a description of the human populations and environmental areas at risk from the impacts of ship emissions;

**.4** an assessment that emissions from ships operating in the proposed area of application are contributing to ambient concentrations of air pollution or to adverse environmental impacts. Such assessment shall include a description of the impacts of the relevant emissions on human health and the environment, such as adverse impacts to terrestrial and aquatic ecosystems, areas of natural productivity, critical habitats, water quality, human health, and areas of cultural and scientific significance, if applicable. The sources of relevant data including methodologies used shall be identified;

**.5** relevant information, pertaining to the meteorological conditions in the proposed area of application, to the human populations and environmental areas at risk, in particular prevailing wind patterns, or to topographical, geological, oceanographic, morphological or other conditions that contribute to ambient concentrations of air pollution or adverse environmental impacts;

**.6** the nature of the ship traffic in the proposed emission control area, including the patterns and density of such traffic;

**.7** a description of the control measures taken by the proposing Party or Parties addressing land-based sources of $NO_x$, $SO_x$ and particulate matter emissions affecting the human populations and environmental areas at risk that are in place and operating concurrent with the consideration of measures to be adopted in relation to provisions of regulations 13 and 14 of Annex VI; and

**.8** the relative costs of reducing emissions from ships when compared with land-based controls, and the economic impacts on shipping engaged in international trade.

**3.2** The geographical limits of an emission control area will be based on the relevant criteria outlined above, including emissions and deposition from ships navigating in the proposed area, traffic patterns and density, and wind conditions.

**4** *Procedures for the assessment and adoption of emission control areas by the Organization*

**4.1** The Organization shall consider each proposal submitted to it by a Party or Parties.

**4.2** In assessing the proposal, the Organization shall take into account the criteria that are to be included in each proposal for adoption as set forth in section 3 above.

**4.3** An emission control area shall be designated by means of an amendment to this Annex, considered, adopted and brought into force in accordance with article 16 of the present Convention.

**5** *Operation of emission control areas*

**5.1** Parties that have ships navigating in the area are encouraged to bring to the Organization any concerns regarding the operation of the area.

# *Appendix IV*

## Type approval and operating limits for shipboard incinerators (Regulation 16)

**1** Shipboard incinerators described in regulation 16.6.1 shall possess an IMO Type Approval Certificate for each incinerator. In order to obtain such certificate, the incinerator shall be designed and built to an approved standard as described in regulation 16.6.1. Each model shall be subject to a specified type approval test operation at the factory or an approved test facility, and under the responsibility of the Administration, using the following standard fuel/waste specification for the type approval test for determining whether the incinerator operates within the limits specified in paragraph 2 of this appendix:

| | |
|---|---|
| Sludge oil consisting of: | 75% sludge oil from heavy fuel oil (HFO);<br>5% waste lubricating oil; and<br>20% emulsified water. |
| Solid waste consisting of: | 50% food waste;<br>50% rubbish containing;<br>approx. 30% paper,<br>" 40% cardboard,<br>" 10% rags,<br>" 20% plastic<br>The mixture will have up to 50% moisture and 7% incombustible solids. |

**2** Incinerators described in regulation 16.6.1 shall operate within the following limits:

| | |
|---|---|
| $O_2$ in combustion chamber: | 6–12% |
| CO in flue gas maximum average: | 200 mg/MJ |
| Soot number maximum average: | Bacharach 3 or<br>Ringelman 1 (20% opacity) (a higher soot number is acceptable only during very short periods such as starting up) |
| Unburned components in ash residues: | Maximum 10% by weight |
| Combustion chamber flue gas outlet temperature range: | 850–1200°C |

# *Appendix V*

## Information to be included in the bunker delivery note (Regulation 18.5)

Name and IMO Number of receiving ship

Port

Date of commencement of delivery

Name, address and telephone number of marine fuel oil supplier

Product name(s)

Quantity in metric tonnes

Density at 15°C, $kg/m^3$*

Sulphur content (% m/m)†

A declaration signed and certified by the fuel oil supplier's representative that the fuel oil supplied is in conformity with the applicable paragraph of regulation 14.1 or 14.4 and regulation 18.3 of this Annex.

* Fuel oil shall be tested in accordance with ISO 3675:1998 or ISO 12185:1996.

† Fuel oil shall be tested in accordance with ISO 8754:2003.

# *Appendix VI*

## Fuel verification procedure for MARPOL Annex VI fuel oil samples (Regulation 18.8.2)

The following procedure shall be used to determine whether the fuel oil delivered to and used on board ships is compliant with the sulphur limits required by regulation 14 of Annex VI.

**1** *General requirements*

**1.1** The representative fuel oil sample, which is required by paragraph 8.1 of regulation 18 (the "MARPOL sample") shall be used to verify the sulphur content of the fuel oil supplied to a ship.

**1.2** An Administration, through its competent authority, shall manage the verification procedure.

**1.3** The laboratories responsible for the verification procedure set forth in this appendix shall be fully accredited* for the purpose of conducting the tests.

**2** *Verification procedure stage 1*

**2.1** The MARPOL sample shall be delivered by the competent authority to the laboratory.

**2.2** The laboratory shall:

- **.1** record the details of the seal number and the sample label on the test record;
- **.2** confirm that the condition of the seal on the MARPOL sample is that it has not been broken; and
- **.3** reject any MARPOL sample where the seal has been broken.

**2.3** If the seal of the MARPOL sample has not been broken, the laboratory shall proceed with the verification procedure and shall:

- **.1** ensure that the MARPOL sample is thoroughly homogenized;

* Accreditation is in accordance with ISO 17025 or an equivalent standard.

**.2** draw two subsamples from the MARPOL sample; and

**.3** reseal the MARPOL sample and record the new reseal details on the test record.

**2.4** The two subsamples shall be tested in succession, in accordance with the specified test method referred to in appendix V (second footnote). For the purposes of this verification procedure, the results of the test analysis shall be referred to as "A" and "B":

**.1** If the results of "A" and "B" are within the repeatability (*r*) of the test method, the results shall be considered valid.

**.2** If the results of "A" and "B" are not within the repeatability (*r*) of the test method, both results shall be rejected and two new subsamples should be taken by the laboratory and analysed. The sample bottle should be resealed in accordance with paragraph 2.3.3 above after the new subsamples have been taken.

**2.5** If the test results of "A" and "B" are valid, an average of these two results should be calculated thus giving the result referred to as "X":

**.1** If the result of "X" is equal to or falls below the applicable limit required by Annex VI, the fuel oil shall be deemed to meet the requirements.

**.2** If the result of "X" is greater than the applicable limit required by Annex VI, verification procedure stage 2 should be conducted; however, if the result of "X" is greater than the specification limit by 0.59*R* (where *R* is the reproducibility of the test method), the fuel oil shall be considered non-compliant and no further testing is necessary.

**3** *Verification procedure stage 2*

**3.1** If stage 2 of the verification procedure is necessary in accordance with paragraph 2.5.2 above, the competent authority shall send the MARPOL sample to a second accredited laboratory.

**3.2** Upon receiving the MARPOL sample, the laboratory shall:

**.1** record the details of the reseal number applied in accordance with 2.3.3 above and the sample label on the test record;

**.2** draw two subsamples from the MARPOL sample; and

**.3** reseal the MARPOL sample and record the new reseal details on the test record.

**3.3** The two subsamples shall be tested in succession, in accordance with the test method specified in appendix V (second footnote). For the purposes of this verification procedure, the results of the test analysis shall be referred to as "C" and "D":

**.1** If the results of "C" and "D" are within the repeatability (*r*) of the test method, the results shall be considered valid.

**.2** If the results of "C" and "D" are not within the repeatability (*r*) of the test method, both results shall be rejected and two new subsamples shall be taken by the laboratory and analysed. The sample bottle should be resealed in accordance with paragraph 3.2.3 above after the new subsamples have been taken.

**3.4** If the test results of "C" and "D" are valid, and the results of "A", "B", "C", and "D" are within the reproducibility (*R*) of the test method then the laboratory shall average the results, which is referred to as "Y":

**.1** If the result of "Y" is equal to or falls below the applicable limit required by Annex VI, the fuel oil shall be deemed to meet the requirements.

**.2** If the result of "Y" is greater than the applicable limit required by Annex VI, then the fuel oil fails to meet the standards required by Annex VI.

**3.5** If the results of "A", "B", "C" and "D" are not within the reproducibility (*R*) of the test method then the Administration may discard all of the test results and, at its discretion, repeat the entire testing process.

**3.6** The results obtained from the verification procedure are final.

# $NO_x$ TECHNICAL CODE 2008

## Technical Code on Control of Emission of Nitrogen Oxides from Marine Diesel Engines

# $NO_x$ Technical Code 2008

*Technical Code on Control of Emission of Nitrogen Oxides from Marine Diesel Engines*

## Contents

## CHAPTER 5 – PROCEDURES FOR $NO_x$ EMISSION MEASUREMENTS ON A TEST BED



## CHAPTER 6 – PROCEDURES FOR DEMONSTRATING COMPLIANCE WITH $NO_x$ EMISSION LIMITS ON BOARD





## APPENDICES

# Introduction

## $NO_x$ Technical Code 2008

On 26 September 1997, the Conference of Parties to the International Convention for the Prevention of Pollution from Ships, 1973, as modified by the Protocol of 1978 relating thereto (MARPOL 73/78) adopted, by Conference resolution 2, the Technical Code on Control of Emission of Nitrogen Oxides from Marine Diesel Engines ($NO_x$ Technical Code). Following the entry into force, on 19 May 2005, of MARPOL Annex VI – Regulations for the Prevention of Air Pollution from Ships, each marine diesel engine to which regulation 13 of that Annex applies must comply with the provisions of this Code. MEPC 53 in July 2005 agreed to the revision of MARPOL Annex VI and the $NO_x$ Technical Code. That review was concluded at MEPC 58 in October 2008 and this version of the $NO_x$ Technical Code, hereunder referred to as the Code, is an outcome of that process.

As general background information, the precursors to the formation of nitrogen oxides during the combustion process are nitrogen and oxygen. Together these compounds compose 99% of the engine intake air. Oxygen will be consumed during the combustion process, with the amount of excess oxygen available being a function of the air/fuel ratio under which the engine is operating. The nitrogen remains largely unreacted in the combustion process; however, a small percentage will be oxidized to form various oxides of nitrogen. The nitrogen oxides ($NO_x$) that can be formed include nitric oxide (NO) and nitrogen dioxide ($NO_2$), while the amounts are primarily a function of flame or combustion temperature and, if present, the amount of organic nitrogen available from the fuel. $NO_x$ formation is also a function of the time the nitrogen and the excess oxygen are exposed to the high temperatures associated with the diesel engine's combustion process. In other words, the higher the combustion temperature (e.g., high peak pressure, high compression ratio, high rate of fuel delivery, etc.), the greater the amount of $NO_x$ formation. A slow-speed diesel engine, in general, tends to have more $NO_x$ formation than a high-speed engine. $NO_x$ has an adverse effect on the environment, causing acidification, formation of tropospheric ozone and nutrient enrichment, and contributes to adverse health effects globally.

The purpose of this Code is to provide mandatory procedures for the testing, survey and certification of marine diesel engines that will enable engine manufacturers, shipowners and Administrations to ensure that all applicable marine diesel engines comply with the relevant limiting emission values of $NO_x$ as specified within regulation 13 of Annex VI. The difficulties of establishing, with precision, the actual weighted average $NO_x$ emission of marine diesel engines in service on ships have been recognized in formulating a simple, practical set of requirements in which the means to ensure compliance with the allowable $NO_x$ emissions are defined.

Administrations are encouraged to assess the emissions performance of marine propulsion and auxiliary diesel engines on a test bed where accurate tests can be carried out under properly controlled conditions. Establishing compliance with regulation 13 of Annex VI at this initial stage is an essential feature of this Code. Subsequent testing on board the ship may inevitably be limited in scope and accuracy, and its purpose shall be to infer or deduce the emission performance and to confirm that engines are installed, operated and maintained in accordance with the manufacturer's specifications and that any adjustments or modifications do not detract from the emissions performance established by initial testing and certification by the manufacturer.

## Abbreviations, subscripts and symbols

Tables 1, 2, 3 and 4 below summarize the abbreviations, subscripts and symbols used throughout this Code, including specifications for the analytical instruments in appendix III, calibration requirements for the analytic instruments contained in appendix IV, the formulae for calculation of gas mass flow as contained in chapter 5 and appendix VI of this Code and the symbols used in respect of data for on-board verification surveys in chapter 6.

- **.1** Table 1: symbols used to represent the chemical components of diesel engine gas emissions and calibration and span gases addressed throughout this Code;
- **.2** Table 2: abbreviations for the analysers used in the measurement of gas emissions from diesel engines as specified in appendix III of this Code;

**.3** Table 3: symbols and subscripts of terms and variables used in chapter 5, chapter 6, appendix IV and appendix VI of this Code; and

**.4** Table 4: symbols for fuel composition used in chapter 5 and chapter 6 and appendix VI of this Code.

*Table 1* – Symbols and abbreviations for the chemical components

| **Symbol** | **Definition** |
|---|---|
| $CH_4$ | Methane |
| $C_3H_8$ | Propane |
| CO | Carbon monoxide |
| $CO_2$ | Carbon dioxide |
| HC | Hydrocarbons |
| $H_2O$ | Water |
| NO | Nitric oxide |
| $NO_2$ | Nitrogen dioxide |
| $NO_x$ | Nitrogen oxides |
| $O_2$ | Oxygen |

*Table 2* – Abbreviations for analysers for measurement of diesel engine gaseous emissions (refer to appendix III of this Code)

| | |
|---|---|
| CLD | Chemiluminescent detector |
| ECS | Electrochemical sensor |
| HCLD | Heated chemiluminescent detector |
| HFID | Heated flame ionization detector |
| NDIR | Non-dispersive infrared analyser |
| PMD | Paramagnetic detector |
| ZRDO | Zirconium dioxide sensor |

*Table 3* – Symbols and subscripts for terms and variables (refer to chapter 5, chapter 6, appendix IV and appendix VI of this Code)

| Symbol | Term | Unit |
|---|---|---|
| $A/F_{st}$ | Stoichiometric air to fuel ratio | 1 |
| $c_x$ | Concentration in the exhaust (with suffix of the component nominating, d = dry or w = wet) | ppm/% (V/V) |
| $E_{CO_2}$ | $CO_2$ quench of $NO_x$ analyser | % |
| $E_{H_2O}$ | Water quench of $NO_x$ analyser | % |
| $E_{NO_x}$ | Efficiency of $NO_x$ converter | % |
| $E_{O_2}$ | Oxygen analyser correction factor | 1 |
| $\lambda$ | Excess air factor: kg dry air/(kg fuel · $A/F_{st}$) | 1 |
| $f_a$ | Test condition parameter | 1 |
| $f_c$ | Carbon factor | 1 |
| $f_{fd}$ | Fuel-specific factor for exhaust flow calculation on dry basis | 1 |
| $f_{fw}$ | Fuel-specific factor for exhaust flow calculation on wet basis | 1 |
| $H_a$ | Absolute humidity of the intake air (g water/kg dry air) | g/kg |
| $H_{SC}$ | Humidity of the charge air | g/kg |
| $i$ | Subscript denoting an individual mode | 1 |
| $k_{hd}$ | Humidity correction factor for $NO_x$ for diesel engines | 1 |
| $k_{wa}$ | Dry to wet correction factor for the intake air | 1 |
| $k_{wr}$ | Dry to wet correction factor for the raw exhaust gas | 1 |
| $n_d$ | Engine speed | $min^{-1}$ |
| $n_{turb}$ | Turbocharger speed | $min^{-1}$ |
| $\%O_2I$ | HC analyser percentage oxygen interference | % |

| Symbol | Term | Unit |
|---|---|---|
| $p_a$ | Saturation vapour pressure of the engine intake air determined using a temperature value for the intake air measured at the same physical location as the measurements for $p_b$ and $R_a$ | kPa |
| $p_b$ | Total barometric pressure | kPa |
| $p_C$ | Charge air pressure | kPa |
| $p_r$ | Water vapour pressure after cooling bath of the analysis system | kPa |
| $p_s$ | Dry atmospheric pressure calculated by the following formula: $p_s = p_b - 0.01 \cdot R_a \cdot p_a$ | kPa |
| $p_{SC}$ | Saturation vapour pressure of the charge air | kPa |
| $P$ | Uncorrected brake power | kW |
| $P_{aux}$ | Declared total power absorbed by auxiliaries fitted for the test and not required by ISO 14396 | kW |
| $P_m$ | Maximum measured or declared power at the test engine speed under test conditions | kW |
| $q_{mad}$ | Intake air mass flow rate on dry basis | kg/h |
| $q_{maw}$ | Intake air mass flow rate on wet basis | kg/h |
| $q_{mew}$ | Exhaust gas mass flow rate on wet basis | kg/h |
| $q_{mf}$ | Fuel mass flow rate | kg/h |
| $q_{mgas}$ | Emission mass flow rate of individual gas | g/h |
| $R_a$ | Relative humidity of the intake air | % |
| $r_h$ | Hydrocarbon response factor | 1 |
| $\rho$ | Density | kg/m$^3$ |
| $s$ | Fuel rack position | |
| $T_a$ | Intake air temperature determined at the engine intake | K |
| $T_{caclin}$ | Charge air cooler, coolant inlet temperature | °C |
| $T_{caclout}$ | Charge air cooler, coolant outlet temperature | °C |
| $T_{Exh}$ | Exhaust gas temperature | °C |

| Symbol | Term | Unit |
|---|---|---|
| $T_{Fuel}$ | Fuel oil temperature | °C |
| $T_{Sea}$ | Seawater temperature | °C |
| $T_{SC}$ | Charge air temperature | K |
| $T_{SCRef}$ | Charge air reference temperature | K |
| $u$ | Ratio of exhaust component and exhaust gas densities | 1 |
| $W_F$ | Weighting factor | 1 |

*Table 4* – Symbols for fuel composition

| Symbol | Definition | Unit |
|---|---|---|
| $w_{ALF}$ | H content of fuel | % m/m |
| $w_{BET}$ | C content of fuel | % m/m |
| $w_{GAM}$ | S content of fuel | % m/m |
| $w_{DEL}$ | N content of fuel | % m/m |
| $w_{EPS}$ | O content of fuel | % m/m |
| $\alpha$ | Molar ratio (H/C) | 1 |

## Resolution MEPC.177(58)

*(adopted on 10 October 2008)*

## AMENDMENTS TO THE TECHNICAL CODE ON CONTROL OF EMISSION OF NITROGEN OXIDES FROM MARINE DIESEL ENGINES ($NO_x$ Technical Code 2008)

THE MARINE ENVIRONMENT PROTECTION COMMITTEE,

RECALLING Article 38(a) of the Convention on the International Maritime Organization concerning the functions of the Marine Environment Protection Committee (the Committee) conferred upon it by international conventions for the prevention and control of marine pollution,

NOTING article 16 of the International Convention for the Prevention of Pollution from Ships, 1973 (hereinafter referred to as the "1973 Convention"), article VI of the Protocol of 1978 relating to the International Convention for the Prevention of Pollution from Ships, 1973 (hereinafter referred to as the "1978 Protocol") and article 4 of the Protocol of 1997 to amend the International Convention for the Prevention of Pollution from Ships, 1973, as modified by the Protocol of 1978 relating thereto (hereinafter referred to as the "1997 Protocol"), which together specify the amendment procedure of the 1997 Protocol and confer upon the appropriate body of the Organization the function of considering and adopting amendments to the 1973 Convention, as modified by the 1978 and 1997 Protocols,

NOTING ALSO that, by the 1997 Protocol, Annex VI entitled Regulations for the Prevention of Air Pollution from Ships is added to the 1973 Convention (hereinafter referred to as "Annex VI"),

NOTING FURTHER regulation 13 of MARPOL Annex VI which makes the Technical Code on Control of Emission of Nitrogen Oxides from

Marine Diesel Engines ($NO_x$ Technical Code) mandatory under that Annex,

HAVING CONSIDERED the draft amendments to the $NO_x$ Technical Code,

1. ADOPTS, in accordance with article 16(2)(d) of the 1973 Convention, the amendments to the $NO_x$ Technical Code, as set out at annex to the present resolution;

2. DETERMINES, in accordance with article 16(2)(f)(iii) of the 1973 Convention, that the amendments shall be deemed to have been accepted on 1 January 2010, unless prior to that date, not less than one-third of the Parties or Parties the combined merchant fleets of which constitute not less than 50 per cent of the gross tonnage of the world's merchant fleet, have communicated to the Organization their objection to the amendments;

3. INVITES the Parties to note that, in accordance with article 16(2)(g)(ii) of the 1973 Convention, the said amendments shall enter into force on 1 July 2010 upon their acceptance in accordance with paragraph 2 above;

4. REQUESTS the Secretary-General, in conformity with article 16(2)(e) of the 1973 Convention, to transmit to all Parties to the 1973 Convention, as modified by the 1978 and 1997 Protocols, certified copies of the present resolution and the text of the amendments contained in the Annex;

5. REQUESTS FURTHER the Secretary-General to transmit to the Members of the Organization which are not Parties to the 1973 Convention, as modified by the 1978 and 1997 Protocols, copies of the present resolution and its Annex;

6. INVITES the Parties to MARPOL Annex VI and other Member Governments to bring the amendments to the $NO_x$ Technical Code to the attention of shipowners, ship operators, shipbuilders, marine diesel engine manufacturers and any other interested groups.

# Chapter 1

## *General*

### 1.1 Purpose

**1.1.1** The purpose of this Technical Code on Control of Emission of Nitrogen Oxides from Marine Diesel Engines, hereunder referred to as the Code, is to specify the requirements for the testing, survey and certification of marine diesel engines to ensure they comply with the nitrogen oxides ($NO_x$) emission limits of regulation 13 of Annex VI. All references to regulations within this Code refer to Annex VI.

### 1.2 Application

**1.2.1** This Code applies to all marine diesel engines with a power output of more than 130 kW that are installed, or are designed and intended for installation, on board any ship subject to Annex VI and to which regulation 13 applies. Regarding the requirements for survey and certification under regulation 5, this Code addresses only those requirements applicable to an engine's compliance with the applicable $NO_x$ emission limit.

**1.2.2** For the purpose of the application of this Code, Administrations are entitled to delegate all functions required of an Administration by this Code to an organization authorized to act on behalf of the Administration.* In every case, the Administration assumes full responsibility for the survey and certificate.

**1.2.3** For the purpose of this Code, an engine shall be considered to be operated in compliance with the applicable $NO_x$ limit of regulation 13 if it can be demonstrated that the weighted $NO_x$ emissions from the engine are within those limits at the initial certification, annual, intermediate and renewal surveys and such other surveys as are required.

* Refer to the Guidelines for the authorization of organizations acting on behalf of the Administration adopted by the Organization by resolution A.739(18) and to the Specifications on the survey and certification functions of recognized organizations acting on behalf of the Administration adopted by the Organization by resolution A.789(19).

## 1.3 Definitions

**1.3.1** *Nitrogen Oxide ($NO_x$) emissions* means the total emission of nitrogen oxides, calculated as the total weighted emission of $NO_2$ and determined using the relevant test cycles and measurement methods as specified in this Code.

**1.3.2** *Substantial modification* of a marine diesel engine means:

**.1** For engines installed on ships constructed on or after 1 January 2000, *substantial modification* means any modification to an engine that could potentially cause the engine to exceed the applicable emission limit set out in regulation 13. Routine replacement of engine components by parts specified in the technical file that do not alter emission characteristics shall not be considered a "substantial modification" regardless of whether one part or many parts are replaced.

**.2** For engines installed on ships constructed before 1 January 2000, *substantial modification* means any modification made to an engine that increases its existing emission characteristics established by the simplified measurement method as described in 6.3 in excess of the allowances set out in 6.3.11. These changes include, but are not limited to, changes in its operations or in its technical parameters (e.g., changing camshafts, fuel injection systems, air systems, combustion chamber configuration, or timing calibration of the engine). The installation of a certified approved method pursuant to regulation 13.7.1.1 or certification pursuant to regulation 13.7.1.2 is not considered to be a substantial modification for the purpose of the application of regulation 13.2 of the Annex.

**1.3.3** *Components* are those interchangeable parts that influence the $NO_x$ emission performance, identified by their design/parts number.

**1.3.4** *Setting* means adjustment of an adjustable feature influencing the $NO_x$ emission performance of an engine.

**1.3.5** *Operating values* are engine data, such as cylinder peak pressure, exhaust gas temperature, etc., from the engine log that are related to the $NO_x$ emission performance. These data are load-dependent.

**1.3.6** The *EIAPP Certificate* is the Engine International Air Pollution Prevention Certificate, which relates to $NO_x$ emissions.

**1.3.7** The *IAPP Certificate* is the International Air Pollution Prevention Certificate.

**1.3.8** *Administration* has the same meaning as article 2, subparagraph (5) of MARPOL 73.

**1.3.9** *On-board* $NO_x$ *verification procedures* means a procedure, which may include an equipment requirement, to be used on board at initial certification survey or at the renewal, annual or intermediate surveys, as required, to verify compliance with any of the requirements of this Code, as specified by the applicant for engine certification and approved by the Administration.

**1.3.10** *Marine diesel engine* means any reciprocating internal combustion engine operating on liquid or dual fuel, to which regulation 13 applies, including booster/compound systems if applied.

Where an engine is intended to be operated normally in the gas mode, i.e., with the main fuel gas and only a small amount of liquid pilot fuel, the requirements of regulation 13 have to be met only for this operation mode. Operation on pure liquid fuel resulting from restricted gas supply in cases of failures shall be exempted for the voyage to the next appropriate port for the repair of the failure.

**1.3.11** *Rated power* means the maximum continuous rated power output as specified on the nameplate and in the technical file of the marine diesel engine to which regulation 13 and this Code apply.

**1.3.12** *Rated speed* is the crankshaft revolutions per minute at which the rated power occurs as specified on the nameplate and in the technical file of the marine diesel engine.

**1.3.13** *Brake power* is the observed power measured at the crankshaft or its equivalent, the engine being equipped only with the standard auxiliaries necessary for its operation on the test bed.

**1.3.14** *On-board conditions* means that an engine is:

- **.1** installed on board and coupled with the actual equipment that is driven by the engine; and
- **.2** under operation to perform the purpose of the equipment.

**1.3.15** A *technical file* is a record containing all details of parameters, including components and settings of an engine, that may influence the $NO_x$ emission of the engine, in accordance with 2.4 of this Code.

**1.3.16** A *record book of engine parameters* is the document used in connection with the engine parameter check method for recording all parameter changes, including components and engine settings, that may influence $NO_x$ emission of the engine.

**1.3.17** An *approved method* is a method for a particular engine, or a range of engines, that, when applied to the engine, will ensure that the engine complies with the applicable $NO_x$ limit as detailed in regulation 13.7.

**1.3.18** An *existing engine* is an engine that is subject to regulation 13.7.

**1.3.19** An *approved method file* is a document that describes an approved method and its means of survey.

# Chapter 2

## *Surveys and certification*

### 2.1 General

**2.1.1** Each marine diesel engine specified in 1.2, except as otherwise permitted by this Code, shall be subject to the following surveys:

**.1** A pre-certification survey that shall be such as to ensure that the engine, as designed and equipped, complies with the applicable $NO_x$ emission limit contained in regulation 13. If this survey confirms compliance, the Administration shall issue an Engine International Air Pollution Prevention (EIAPP) Certificate.

**.2** An initial certification survey that shall be conducted on board a ship after the engine is installed but before it is placed in service. This survey shall be such as to ensure that the engine, as installed on board the ship, including any modifications and/or adjustments since the pre-certification, if applicable, complies with the applicable $NO_x$ emission limit contained in regulation 13. This survey, as part of the ship's initial survey, may lead to either the issuance of a ship's initial International Air Pollution Prevention (IAPP) Certificate or an amendment of a ship's valid IAPP Certificate reflecting the installation of a new engine.

**.3** Renewal, annual and intermediate surveys, which shall be conducted as part of a ship's surveys required by regulation 5, to ensure the engine continues to comply fully with the provisions of this Code.

**.4** An initial engine certification survey that shall be conducted on board a ship every time a major conversion, as defined in regulation 13, is made to an engine, to ensure that the engine complies with the applicable $NO_x$ emission limit contained in regulation 13. This will result in the issue, if applicable, of an EIAPP Certificate and the amendment of the IAPP Certificate.

**2.1.2** To comply with the various survey and certification requirements described in 2.1.1, there are methods included in this Code from which the engine manufacturer, shipbuilder or shipowner, as applicable, can choose to measure, calculate, test or verify an engine for its $NO_x$ emissions, as follows:

**.1** test-bed testing for the pre-certification survey in accordance with chapter 5;

**.2** on-board testing for an engine not pre-certificated for a combined pre-certification and initial certification survey in accordance with the full test-bed requirements of chapter 5;

**.3** on-board engine parameter check method, using the component data, engine settings and engine performance data as specified in the technical file, for confirmation of compliance at initial, renewal, annual and intermediate surveys for pre-certified engines or engines that have undergone modifications or adjustments to $NO_x$ critical components, settings and operating values since they were last surveyed, in accordance with 6.2;

**.4** on-board simplified measurement method for confirmation of compliance at renewal, annual and intermediate surveys or confirmation of pre-certified engines for initial certification surveys, in accordance with 6.3 when required; or

**.5** on-board direct measurement and monitoring method for confirmation of compliance at renewal, annual and intermediate surveys only, in accordance with 6.4.

## 2.2 Procedures for pre-certification of an engine

**2.2.1** Prior to installation on board, every marine diesel engine (individual engine), except as allowed by 2.2.2 and 2.2.4, shall:

**.1** be adjusted to meet the applicable $NO_x$ emission limit,

**.2** have its $NO_x$ emissions measured on a test bed in accordance with the procedures specified in chapter 5 of this Code, and

**.3** be pre-certified by the Administration, as documented by issuance of an EIAPP Certificate.

**2.2.2** For the pre-certification of serially manufactured engines, depending on the approval of the Administration, the engine family or the engine group concept may be applied (see chapter 4). In such a case, the testing specified in 2.2.1.2 is required only for the parent engine(s) of an engine family or engine group.

**2.2.3** The method of obtaining pre-certification for an engine is for the Administration to:

**.1** certify a test of the engine on a test bed;

**.2** verify that all engines tested, including, if applicable, those to be delivered within an engine family or engine group, meet the applicable $NO_x$ limit; and

**.3** if applicable, verify that the selected parent engine(s) is representative of an engine family or engine group.

**2.2.4** There are engines that, due to their size, construction and delivery schedule, cannot be pre-certified on a test bed. In such cases, the engine manufacturer, shipowner or shipbuilder shall make application to the Administration requesting an on-board test (see 2.1.2.2). The applicant must demonstrate to the Administration that the on-board test fully meets all of the requirements of a test-bed procedure as specified in chapter 5 of this Code. Such a survey may be accepted for an individual engine or for an engine group represented by the parent engine only, but it shall not be accepted for an engine family certification. In no case shall an allowance be granted for possible deviations of measurements if an initial survey is carried out on board a ship without any valid pre-certification test. For engines undergoing an on-board certification test, in order to be issued with an EIAPP Certificate, the same procedures apply as if the engine had been pre-certified on a test bed.

**2.2.5** *$NO_x$-reducing devices*

**.1** Where an $NO_x$-reducing device is to be included within the EIAPP certification, it must be recognized as a component of the engine and its presence shall be recorded in the engine's technical file. The engine shall be tested, at the pre-certification test, with the $NO_x$-reducing device fitted.

**.2** In those cases where an $NO_x$-reducing device has been fitted due to failure to meet the required emission value at the pre-certification test, in order to receive an EIAPP Certificate for this assembly, the engine, including the reducing device, as installed, must be re-tested to show compliance with the applicable $NO_x$ emission limit. However, in this case, the assembly may be re-tested in accordance with the simplified measurement method in accordance with 6.3. In no case shall the allowances given in 6.3.11 be granted.

**.3** Where, in accordance with 2.2.5.2, the effectiveness of the $NO_x$-reducing device is verified by use of the simplified measurement method, that test report shall be added as an adjunct to the pre-certification test report that demonstrated the failure of the engine alone to meet the required emission value. Both test reports shall be submitted to the Administration, and test report data, as detailed in 2.4.1.5, covering both tests shall be included in the engine's technical file.

**.4** The simplified measurement method used as part of the process to demonstrate compliance in accordance with 2.2.5.2 may only be accepted in respect of the engine and $NO_x$-reducing device on which its effectiveness was demonstrated, and it shall not be accepted for engine family or engine group certification.

**.5** In both cases as given in 2.2.5.1 and 2.2.5.2, the $NO_x$-reducing device shall be included on the EIAPP Certificate together with the emission value obtained with the device in operation and all other records as required by the Administration. The engine's technical file shall also contain on-board $NO_x$ verification procedures for the device to ensure it is operating correctly.

**.6** Notwithstanding 2.2.5.3 and 2.2.5.4, an $NO_x$-reducing device may be approved by the Administration taking into account guidelines to be developed by the Organization.

**2.2.6** Where, due to changes of component design, it is necessary to establish a new engine family or engine group but there is no available parent engine, the engine builder may apply to the Administration to use the previously obtained parent engine test data modified at each specific mode of the applicable test cycle so as to allow for the resulting changes in $NO_x$ emission values. In such cases, the engine used to determine the modification emission data shall correspond in accordance with the requirements of 4.4.6.1, 4.4.6.2 and 4.4.6.3 to the previously used parent engine. Where more than one component is to be changed the combined effect resulting from those changes is to be demonstrated by a single set of test results.

**2.2.7** For pre-certification of engines within an engine family or engine group, an EIAPP Certificate shall be issued in accordance with procedures established by the Administration to the parent engine(s) and to every member engine produced under this certification to accompany the engines throughout their life whilst installed on ships under the authority of that Administration.

**2.2.8** *Issue of certification by the Administration of the country in which the engine is built*

**.1** When an engine is manufactured outside the country of the Administration of the ship on which it will be installed, the Administration of the ship may request the Administration of the country in which the engine is manufactured to survey the engine. Upon satisfaction that the applicable requirements of regulation 13 are complied with pursuant to this Code, the Administration of the country in which the engine is manufactured shall issue or authorize the issuance of the EIAPP Certificate.

**.2** A copy of the certificate(s) and a copy of the survey report shall be transmitted as soon as possible to the requesting Administration.

**.3** A certificate so issued shall contain a statement to the effect that it has been issued at the request of the Administration.

**2.2.9** Guidance in respect of the pre-certification survey and certification of marine diesel engines, as described in chapter 2 of this Code, is given in the relevant flowchart in appendix II of this Code. Where discrepancies exist, the text of chapter 2 takes precedence.

**2.2.10** A model form of an EIAPP Certificate is attached as appendix I to this Code.

## 2.3 Procedures for certification of an engine

**2.3.1** For those engines that have not been adjusted or modified relative to the original specification of the manufacturer, the provision of a valid EIAPP Certificate should suffice to demonstrate compliance with the applicable $NO_x$ limits.

**2.3.2** After installation on board, it shall be determined to what extent an engine has been subjected to further adjustments and/or modifications that could affect the $NO_x$ emission. Therefore, the engine, after installation on board, but prior to issuance of the IAPP Certificate, shall be inspected for modifications and be approved using the on-board $NO_x$ verification procedures and one of the methods described in 2.1.2.

**2.3.3** There are engines that, after pre-certification, need final adjustment or modification for performance. In such a case, the engine group concept could be used to ensure that the engine still complies with the applicable limit.

**2.3.4** Every marine diesel engine installed on board a ship shall be provided with a technical file. The technical file shall be prepared by the applicant for engine certification and approved by the Administration, and is required to accompany an engine throughout its life on board ships. The technical file shall contain the information as specified in 2.4.1.

**2.3.5** Where an $NO_x$-reducing device is installed and needed to comply with the $NO_x$ limits, one of the options providing a ready means for verifying compliance with regulation 13 is the direct measurement and monitoring method in accordance with 6.4. However, depending on the technical possibilities of the device used, subject to the approval of the Administration, other relevant parameters could be monitored.

**2.3.6** Where, for the purpose of achieving $NO_x$ compliance, an additional substance is introduced, such as ammonia, urea, steam, water, fuel additives, etc., a means of monitoring the consumption of such substance shall be provided. The technical file shall provide sufficient information to allow a ready means of demonstrating that the consumption of such additional substances is consistent with achieving compliance with the applicable $NO_x$ limit.

**2.3.7** Where the engine parameter check method in accordance with 6.2 is used to verify compliance, if any adjustments or modifications are made to an engine after its pre-certification, a full record of such adjustments or modifications shall be recorded in the engine's record book of engine parameters.

**2.3.8** If all of the engines installed on board are verified to remain within the parameters, components and adjustable features recorded in the technical file, the engines should be accepted as performing within the applicable $NO_x$ limit specified in regulation 13. In this case, provided all other applicable requirements of the Annex are complied with, an IAPP Certificate should then be issued to the ship.

**2.3.9** If any adjustment or modification is made that is outside the approved limits documented in the technical file, the IAPP Certificate may be issued only if the overall $NO_x$ emission performance is verified to be within the required limits by: on-board simplified measurement in accordance with 6.3; or, reference to the test-bed testing for the relevant engine group approval showing that the adjustments or modifications do not exceed the applicable $NO_x$ emission limit. At surveys after the initial engine survey, the direct measurement and monitoring method in accordance with 6.4, as approved by the Administration, may alternatively be used.

**2.3.10** The Administration may, at its own discretion, abbreviate or reduce all parts of the survey on board, in accordance with this Code, to an engine that has been issued an EIAPP Certificate. However, the entire survey on board must be completed for at least one cylinder and/or one engine in an engine family or engine group, if applicable, and the abbreviation may be made only if all the other cylinders and/or engines are expected to perform in the same manner as the surveyed engine and/or cylinder. As an alternative to the examination of fitted components, the Administration may conduct that part of the survey on spare parts carried on board provided they are representative of the components fitted.

**2.3.11** Guidance in respect of the survey and certification of marine diesel engines at initial, renewal, annual and intermediate surveys, as described in chapter 2 of this Code, is given in the flowcharts in appendix II of this Code. Where discrepancies exist, the text of chapter 2 takes precedence.

## 2.4 Technical file and on-board $NO_x$ verification procedures

**2.4.1** To enable an Administration to perform the engine surveys described in 2.1, the technical file required by 2.3.4 shall, at a minimum, contain the following information:

**.1** identification of those components, settings and operating values of the engine that influence its $NO_x$ emissions including any $NO_x$-reducing device or system;

**.2** identification of the full range of allowable adjustments or alternatives for the components of the engine;

**.3** full record of the relevant engine's performance, including the engine's rated speed and rated power;

**.4** a system of on-board $NO_x$ verification procedures to verify compliance with the $NO_x$ emission limits during on-board verification surveys in accordance with chapter 6;

**.5** a copy of the relevant parent engine test data, as given in section 2 of appendix V of this Code;

**.6** if applicable, the designation and restrictions for an engine that is an engine within an engine family or engine group;

**.7** specifications of those spare parts/components that, when used in the engine, according to those specifications, will result in continued compliance of the engine with the applicable $NO_x$ emission limit; and

**.8** the EIAPP Certificate, as applicable.

**2.4.2** As a general principle, on-board $NO_x$ verification procedures shall enable a surveyor to easily determine if an engine has remained in compliance with the applicable requirements of regulation 13. At the same time, it shall not be so burdensome as to unduly delay the ship or to require in-depth knowledge of the characteristics of a particular engine or specialist measuring devices not available on board.

**2.4.3** The on-board $NO_x$ verification procedure shall be one of the following methods:

**.1** engine parameter check method in accordance with 6.2 to verify that an engine's component, setting and operating values have not deviated from the specifications in the engine's technical file;

**.2** simplified measurement method in accordance with 6.3; or

**.3** direct measurement and monitoring method in accordance with 6.4.

**2.4.4** When considering which on-board $NO_x$ verification procedures should be included in an engine's technical file to verify whether an engine complies with the applicable $NO_x$ emission limit during the required on-board verification surveys, other than at an engine's initial on-board survey, any of the three on-board $NO_x$ verification procedures as specified in 6.1 may be applied. However, the procedures associated with the method applied are to be approved by the Administration. If the method differs from the verification procedure method specified in the technical file as originally approved, the procedure of the method needs to be either added as an amendment to the technical file or appended as an alternative to the procedure given in the technical file. Thereafter the shipowner may choose which of the methods approved in the technical file is to be used to demonstrate compliance.

**2.4.5** In addition to the method specified by the engine manufacturer and given in the technical file, as approved by the Administration for the initial certification in the engine, the shipowner shall have the option of direct measurement of $NO_x$ emissions in accordance with 6.4. Such data may take the form of spot checks logged with other engine operating data on a regular basis and over the full range of engine operation or may result from continuous monitoring and data storage. Data must be current (taken within the last 30 days) and must have been acquired using the test procedures cited in this Code. These monitoring records shall be kept on board for three months for verification purposes by a Party in accordance with regulation 10. Data shall also be corrected for ambient conditions and fuel specification, and measuring equipment must be checked for correct calibration and operation, in accordance with the approved procedures given in the on-board operating manual. Where exhaust gas after-treatment devices are fitted that influence the $NO_x$ emissions, the measuring point(s) must be located downstream of such devices.

# Chapter 3

## *Nitrogen oxides emission standards*

### 3.1 Maximum allowable $NO_x$ emission limits for marine diesel engines

**3.1.1** The maximum allowable $NO_x$ emission limit values are given by paragraphs 3, 4, 5.1.1 and 7.4 of regulation 13 as applicable. The total weighted $NO_x$ emissions, as measured and calculated, rounded to one decimal place, in accordance with the procedures in this Code, shall be equal to or less than the applicable calculated value corresponding to the rated speed of the engine.

**3.1.2** When the engine operates on test fuel oils in accordance with 5.3, the total emission of nitrogen oxides (calculated as the total weighted emission of $NO_2$) shall be determined using the relevant test cycles and measurement methods as specified in this Code.

**3.1.3** An engine's exhaust emissions limit value, given from the formulae included in paragraph 3, 4 or 5.1.1 of regulation 13 as applicable, and the actual calculated exhaust emissions value, rounded to one decimal place for the engine, shall be stated on the engine's EIAPP Certificate. If an engine is a member engine of an engine family or engine group, it is the relevant parent engine emission value that is compared to the applicable limit value for that engine family or engine group. The limit value given here shall be the limit value for the engine family or engine group based on the highest engine speed to be included in that engine family or engine group, in accordance with paragraph 3, 4 or 5.1.1 of regulation 13, irrespective of the rated speed of the parent engine or the rated speed of the particular engine as given on the engine's EIAPP certificate.

**3.1.4** In the case of an engine to be certified in accordance with paragraph 5.1.1 of regulation 13 the specific emission at each individual mode point shall not exceed the applicable $NO_x$ emission limit value by more than 50% except as follows:

**.1** The 10% mode point in the D2 test cycle specified in 3.2.5.

**.2** The 10% mode point in the C1 test cycle specified in 3.2.6.

**.3** The idle mode point in the C1 test cycle specified in 3.2.6.

## 3.2 Test cycles and weighting factors to be applied

**3.2.1** For every individual engine or parent engine of an engine family or engine group, one or more of the relevant test cycles specified in 3.2.2 to 3.2.6 shall be applied for verification of compliance with the applicable $NO_x$ emission limit contained in regulation 13.

**3.2.2** For constant-speed marine diesel engines for ship main propulsion, including diesel electric drive, test cycle E2 shall be applied in accordance with table 1.

**3.2.3** For an engine connected to a controllable pitch propeller, irrespective of combinator curve, test cycle E2 shall be applied in accordance with table 1.

*Table 1* – Test cycle for "Constant-speed main propulsion" application (including diesel-electric drive and all controllable-pitch propeller installations)

| | | | | | |
|---|---|---|---|---|---|
| Test cycle type E2 | Speed | 100% | 100% | 100% | 100%* |
| | Power | 100% | 75% | 50% | 25% |
| | Weighting factor | 0.2 | 0.5 | 0.15 | 0.15 |

**3.2.4** For propeller-law-operated main and propeller-law-operated auxiliary engines, test cycle E3 shall be applied in accordance with table 2.

*Table 2* – Test cycle for "Propeller-law-operated main and propeller-law-operated auxiliary engine" application

| | | | | | |
|---|---|---|---|---|---|
| Test cycle type E3 | Speed | 100% | 91% | 80% | 63% |
| | Power | 100% | 75% | 50% | 25% |
| | Weighting factor | 0.2 | 0.5 | 0.15 | 0.15 |

* There are exceptional cases, including large bore engines intended for E2 applications, in which, due to their oscillating masses and construction, engines cannot be run at low load at nominal speed without the risk of damaging essential components. In such cases, the engine manufacturer shall make application to the Administration that the test cycle as given in table 1 above may be modified for the 25% power mode with regard to the engine speed. The adjusted engine speed at 25% power, however, shall be as close as possible to the rated engine speed, as recommended by the engine manufacturer and approved by the Administration. The applicable weighting factors for the test cycle shall remain unchanged.

**3.2.5** For constant-speed auxiliary engines, test cycle D2 shall be applied in accordance with table 3.

*Table 3* – Test cycle for "Constant-speed auxiliary engine" application

| | | | | | | |
|---|---|---|---|---|---|---|
| Test cycle type D2 | Speed | 100% | 100% | 100% | 100% | 100% |
| | Power | 100% | 75% | 50% | 25% | 10% |
| | Weighting factor | 0.05 | 0.25 | 0.3 | 0.3 | 0.1 |

**3.2.6** For variable-speed, variable-load auxiliary engines not included above, test cycle C1 shall be applied in accordance with table 4.

*Table 4* – Test cycle for "Variable-speed, variable-load auxiliary engine" application

| | | | | | | | | | |
|---|---|---|---|---|---|---|---|---|---|
| Test cycle type C1 | Speed | Rated | | | | Intermediate | | | Idle |
| | Torque | 100% | 75% | 50% | 10% | 100% | 75% | 50% | 0% |
| | Weighting factor | 0.15 | 0.15 | 0.15 | 0.1 | 0.1 | 0.1 | 0.1 | 0.15 |

**3.2.7** The torque figures given in test cycle C1 are percentage values that represent for a given test mode the ratio of the required torque to the maximum possible torque at this given speed.

**3.2.8** The intermediate speed for test cycle C1 shall be declared by the manufacturer, taking into account the following requirements:

**.1** For engines that are designed to operate over a speed range on a full load torque curve, the intermediate speed shall be the declared maximum torque speed if it occurs between 60% and 75% of rated speed.

**.2** If the declared maximum torque speed is less than 60% of rated speed, then the intermediate speed shall be 60% of the rated speed.

**.3** If the declared maximum torque speed is greater than 75% of the rated speed, then the intermediate speed shall be 75% of rated speed.

**.4** For engines that are not designed to operate over a speed range on the full load torque curve at steady state conditions, the intermediate speed will typically be between 60% and 70% of the maximum rated speed.

**3.2.9** If an engine manufacturer applies for a new test cycle application on an engine already certified under a different test cycle specified in 3.2.2 to 3.2.6, then it may not be necessary for that engine to undergo the full certification process for the new application. In this case, the engine manufacturer may demonstrate compliance by recalculation, by applying the measurement results from the specific modes of the first certification test to the calculation of the total weighted emissions for the new test cycle application, using the corresponding weighting factors from the new test cycle.

# Chapter 4

## *Approval for serially manufactured engines: engine family and engine group concepts*

### 4.1 General

**4.1.1** To avoid certification testing of every engine for compliance with the $NO_x$ emission limits, one of two approval concepts may be adopted, namely the engine family or the engine group concept.

**4.1.2** The engine family concept may be applied to any series-produced engines that, through their design, are proven to have similar $NO_x$ emission characteristics, are used as produced and, during installation on board, require no adjustments or modifications that could adversely affect the $NO_x$ emissions.

**4.1.3** The engine group concept may be applied to a smaller series of engines produced for similar engine application and that require minor adjustments and modifications during installation or in service on board.

**4.1.4** Initially the engine manufacturer may, at its discretion, determine whether engines should be covered by the engine family or engine group concept. In general, the type of application shall be based on whether the engines will be modified, and to what extent, after testing on a test bed.

### 4.2 Documentation

**4.2.1** All documentation for certification must be completed and suitably stamped by the duly authorized Authority as appropriate. This documentation shall also include all terms and conditions, including replacement of spare parts, to ensure that an engine is maintained in compliance with the applicable $NO_x$ emission limit.

**4.2.2** For an engine within an engine family or engine group, the required documentation for the engine parameter check method is specified in 6.2.2.

### 4.3 Application of the engine family concept

**4.3.1** The engine family concept provides the possibility of reducing the number of engines that must be submitted for approval testing, while providing safeguards that all engines within the engine family comply with the approval requirements. In the engine family concept, engines with similar emission characteristics and design are represented by a parent engine.

**4.3.2** Engines that are series-produced and not intended to be modified may be covered by the engine family concept.

**4.3.3** The selection procedure for the parent engine is such that the selected engine incorporates those features that will most adversely affect the $NO_x$ emission level. This engine, in general, shall have the highest $NO_x$ emission level among all of the engines in the engine family.

**4.3.4** On the basis of tests and engineering judgement, the manufacturer shall propose which engines belong to an engine family, which engine(s) produce the highest $NO_x$ emissions, and which engine(s) should be selected for certification testing.

**4.3.5** The Administration shall review for certification approval the selection of the parent engine within the engine family and shall have the option of selecting a different engine, either for approval or production conformity testing, in order to have confidence that all engines within the engine family comply with the applicable $NO_x$ emission limit.

**4.3.6** The engine family concept does allow minor adjustments to the engines through adjustable features. Marine diesel engines equipped with adjustable features must comply with all requirements for any adjustment within the physically available range. A feature is not considered adjustable if it is permanently sealed or otherwise not normally accessible. The Administration may require that adjustable features be set to any specification within its adjustable range for certification or in-use testing to determine compliance with the requirements.

**4.3.7** Before granting an engine family approval, the Administration shall take the necessary measures to verify that adequate arrangements have been made to ensure effective control of the conformity of production. This may include, but is not limited to:

**.1** the connection between the $NO_x$ critical component part or identification numbers as proposed for the engine family and the drawing numbers (and revision status if applicable) defining those components;

**.2** the means by which the Administration will be able, at the time of a survey, to verify that the drawings used for the production of the $NO_x$ critical components correspond to the drawings established as defining the engine family;

**.3** drawing revision control arrangements. Where it is proposed by a manufacturer that revisions to the $NO_x$ critical component drawings defining an engine family may be undertaken through the life of an engine, then the conformity of production scheme would need to demonstrate the procedures to be adopted to cover the cases where revisions will, or will not, affect $NO_x$ emissions. These procedures shall cover drawing number allocation, effect on the identification markings on the $NO_x$ critical components and the provision for providing the revised drawings to the Administration responsible for the original engine family approval. Where these revisions may affect the $NO_x$ emissions, the means to be adopted to assess or verify performance against the parent engine performance are to be stated together with the subsequent actions to be taken regarding advising the Administration and, where necessary, the declaration of a new parent engine prior to the introduction of those modifications into service;

**.4** the implemented procedures that ensure any $NO_x$ critical component spare parts supplied to a certified engine will be identified as given in the approved technical file and hence will be produced in accordance with the drawings as defining the engine family; or

**.5** equivalent arrangements as approved by the Administration.

**4.3.8** *Guidance for the selection of an engine family*

**4.3.8.1** The engine family shall be defined by basic characteristics that must be common to all engines within the engine family. In some cases there may be interaction of parameters; these effects must also be taken into consideration to ensure that only engines with similar exhaust emission characteristics are included within an engine family, e.g., the number of cylinders may become a relevant parameter on some engines due to the charge air or fuel system used, but with other designs, exhaust emissions characteristics may be independent of the number of cylinders or configuration.

**4.3.8.2** The engine manufacturer is responsible for selecting those engines from their different models of engines that are to be included in an engine family. The following basic characteristics, but not specifications, shall be common among all engines within an engine family:

**.1** combustion cycle:
- 2-stroke cycle
- 4-stroke cycle

**.2** cooling medium:
- air
- water
- oil

**.3** individual cylinder displacement:
- to be within a total spread of 15%

**.4** number of cylinders and cylinder configuration:
- applicable in certain cases only, e.g., in combination with exhaust gas cleaning devices

**.5** method of air aspiration:
- naturally aspirated
- pressure charged

**.6** fuel type:
- distillate/residual fuel oil
- dual fuel

**.7** combustion chamber
- open chamber
- divided chamber

**.8** valve and porting, configuration, size and number:
- cylinder head
- cylinder wall

**.9** fuel system type:
- pump-line-injector
- in-line
- distributor
- single element
- unit injector
- gas valve

**.10** miscellaneous features:
- exhaust gas re-circulation
- water/emulsion injection
- air injection
- charge cooling system
- exhaust after-treatment
- reduction catalyst
- oxidation catalyst
- thermal reactor
- particulates trap

**4.3.8.3** If there are engines that incorporate other features that could be considered to affect $NO_x$ exhaust emissions, these features must be identified and taken into account in the selection of the engines to be included in the engine family.

**4.3.9** *Guidance for selecting the parent engine of an engine family*

**4.3.9.1** The method of selection of the parent engine for $NO_x$ measurement shall be agreed to and approved by the Administration. The method shall be based upon selecting an engine that incorporates engine features and characteristics that, from experience, are known to produce the highest $NO_x$ emissions expressed in grams per kilowatt hour (g/kWh). This requires detailed knowledge of the engines within the engine family. Under certain circumstances, the Administration may conclude that the worst case $NO_x$ emission rate of the engine family can best be characterized by testing a second engine. Thus, the Administration may select an additional engine for test based upon features that indicate that it may have the highest $NO_x$ emission levels of the engines within that engine family. If the range of engines within the engine family incorporate other variable features that could be considered to affect $NO_x$ emissions, these features must also be identified and taken into account in the selection of the parent engine.

**4.3.9.2** The parent engine shall have the highest emission value for the applicable test cycle.

**4.3.10** *Certification of an engine family*

**4.3.10.1** The certification shall include a list, to be prepared and maintained by the engine manufacturer and approved by the

Administration, of all engines and their specifications accepted under the same engine family, the limits of their operating conditions and the details and limits of engine adjustments that may be permitted.

**4.3.10.2** A pre-certificate, or EIAPP Certificate, shall be issued for a member engine of an engine family in accordance with this Code that certifies that the parent engine meets the applicable $NO_x$ limit specified in regulation 13. Where member engine pre-certification requires the measurement of some performance values, the calibration of the equipment used for those measurements shall be in accordance with the requirements of 1.3 of appendix IV of this Code.

**4.3.10.3** When the parent engine of an engine family is tested and gaseous emissions measured under the most adverse conditions specified within this Code and confirmed as complying with the applicable maximum allowable emission limits as given in 3.1, the results of the test and $NO_x$ measurement shall be recorded in the EIAPP Certificate issued for the particular parent engine and for all member engines of the engine family.

**4.3.10.4** If two or more Administrations agree to accept each other's EIAPP Certificates, then an entire engine family, certified by one of these Administrations, shall be accepted by the other Administrations that entered into that agreement with the original certifying Administration, unless the agreement specifies otherwise. Certificates issued under such agreements shall be acceptable as prima facie evidence that all engines included in the certification of the engine family comply with the specific $NO_x$ emission requirements. There is no need for further evidence of compliance with regulation 13 if it is verified that the installed engine has not been modified and the engine adjustment is within the range permitted in the engine family certification.

**4.3.10.5** If the parent engine of an engine family is to be certified in accordance with an alternative standard or a different test cycle than allowed by this Code, the manufacturer must prove to the Administration that the weighted average $NO_x$ emissions for the appropriate test cycles fall within the relevant limit values under regulation 13 and this Code before the Administration may issue an EIAPP Certificate.

## 4.4 Application of the engine group concept

**4.4.1** Engine group engines normally require adjustment or modification to suit the on-board operating conditions, but these adjustments or modifications shall not result in $NO_x$ emissions exceeding the applicable limits in regulation 13.

**4.4.2** The engine group concept also provides the possibility for a reduction in approval testing for modifications to engines in production or in service.

**4.4.3** In general, the engine group concept may be applied to any engine type having the same design features as specified in 4.4.6, but individual engine adjustment or modification after test-bed measurement is allowed. The range of engines in an engine group and choice of parent engine shall be agreed to and approved by the Administration.

**4.4.4** The application for the engine group concept, if requested by the engine manufacturer or another party, shall be considered for certification approval by the Administration. If the engine owner, with or without technical support from the engine manufacturer, decides to perform modifications on a number of similar engines in the owner's fleet, the owner may apply for an engine group certification. The engine group may be based on a parent engine that is a test engine on the test bench. Typical applications are similar modifications of similar engines in similar operational conditions. If a party other than the engine manufacturer applies for engine certification, the applicant for the engine certification takes on the responsibilities of the engine manufacturer as elsewhere given within this Code.

**4.4.5** Before granting an initial engine group approval for serially produced engines, the Administration shall take the necessary measures to verify that adequate arrangements have been made to ensure effective control of the conformity of production. The requirements of 4.3.7 apply *mutatis mutandis* to this section. This requirement may not be necessary for engine groups established for the purpose of engine modification on board after an EIAPP Certificate has been issued.

**4.4.6** *Guidance for the selection of an engine group*

**4.4.6.1** The engine group may be defined by basic characteristics and specifications in addition to the parameters defined in 4.3.8 for an engine family.

**4.4.6.2** The following parameters and specifications shall be common to engines within an engine group:

- **.1** bore and stroke dimensions;
- **.2** method and design features of pressure charging and exhaust gas system:
  - – constant pressure;
  - – pulsating system;
- **.3** method of charge air cooling system:
  - – with/without charge air cooler;
- **.4** design features of the combustion chamber that affect $NO_x$ emission;
- **.5** design features of the fuel injection system, plunger and injection cam that may profile basic characteristics that affect $NO_x$ emission; and
- **.6** rated power at rated speed. The permitted ranges of engine power (kW/cylinder) and/or rated speed are to be declared by the manufacturer and approved by the Administration.

**4.4.6.3** Generally, if the criteria required by 4.4.6.2 are not common to all engines within a prospective engine group, then those engines may not be considered as an engine group. However, an engine group may be accepted if only one of those criteria is not common for all of the engines within a prospective engine group.

### 4.4.7 *Guidance for allowable adjustment or modification within an engine group*

**4.4.7.1** Minor adjustments and modifications in accordance with the engine group concept are allowed after pre-certification or final test-bed measurement within an engine group upon agreement of the parties concerned and approval of the Administration, if:

- **.1** an inspection of emission-relevant engine parameters and/or provisions of the on-board $NO_x$ verification procedures of the engine and/or data provided by the engine manufacturer confirm that the adjusted or modified engine complies with the applicable $NO_x$ emission limit. The engine test-bed results in respect of $NO_x$ emissions may be accepted as an option for verifying on-board adjustments or modifications to an engine within an engine group; or

**.2** on-board measurement confirms that the adjusted or modified engine complies with the applicable $NO_x$ emission limit.

**4.4.7.2** Examples of adjustments and modifications within an engine group that may be permitted, but are not limited to those described below:

**.1** For on-board conditions, adjustment of:
- injection timing for compensation of fuel property differences,
- injection timing for maximum cylinder pressure,
- fuel delivery differences between cylinders.

**.2** For performance, modification of:
- turbocharger,
- injection pump components,
- plunger specification,
- delivery valve specification,
- injection nozzles,
- cam profiles,
- intake and/or exhaust valve,
- injection cam,
- combustion chamber.

**4.4.7.3** The above examples of modifications after a test-bed trial concern essential improvements of components or engine performance during the life of an engine. This is one of the main reasons for the existence of the engine group concept. The Administration, upon application, may accept the results from a demonstration test carried out on one engine, possibly a test engine, indicating the effects of the modifications on $NO_x$ emissions that may be accepted for all engines within that engine group without requiring certification measurements on each member engine of the engine group.

**4.4.8** *Guidance for the selection of the parent engine of an engine group*

**4.4.8.1** The selection of the parent engine shall be in accordance with the criteria in 4.3.9, as applicable. It is not always possible to select a parent engine from small-volume production engines in the same way as the mass-produced engines (engine family). The first engine ordered may be registered as the parent engine. Furthermore, at the pre-certification test where a parent engine is not adjusted to the engine-builder-defined reference or maximum tolerance operating conditions (which may include, but are not limited to, maximum combustion pressure, compression pressure, exhaust back pressure, charge air temperature) for the engine group, the measured $NO_x$ emission values shall be corrected to the defined reference and maximum tolerance conditions on the basis of emission sensitivity tests on other representative engines. The resulting corrected average weighted $NO_x$ emission value under reference conditions is to be stated in 1.9.6 of the Supplement to the EIAPP Certificate. In no case is the effect of the reference condition tolerances to result in an emission value that would exceed the applicable $NO_x$ emission limit as required by regulation 13. The method used to select the parent engine to represent the engine group, the reference values and the applied tolerances shall be agreed to and approved by the Administration.

**4.4.9** *Certification of an engine group*

**4.4.9.1** The requirements of 4.3.10 apply *mutatis mutandis* to this section.

# Chapter 5

## *Procedures for $NO_x$ emission measurements on a test bed*

### 5.1 General

**5.1.1** This procedure shall be applied to every initial approval testing of a marine diesel engine regardless of the location of that testing (the methods described in 2.1.2.1 and 2.1.2.2).

**5.1.2** This chapter specifies the measurement and calculation methods for gaseous exhaust emissions from reciprocating internal combustion engines under steady-state conditions, necessary for determining the average weighted value for the $NO_x$ exhaust gas emission.

**5.1.3** Many of the procedures described below are detailed accounts of laboratory methods, since determining an emissions value requires performing a complex set of individual measurements, rather than obtaining a single measured value. Thus, the results obtained depend as much on the process of performing the measurements as they depend on the engine and test method.

**5.1.4** This chapter includes the test and measurement methods, test run and test report as a procedure for a test-bed measurement.

**5.1.5** In principle, during emission tests, an engine shall be equipped with its auxiliaries in the same manner as it would be used on board.

**5.1.6** For many engine types within the scope of this Code, the auxiliaries that may be fitted to the engine in service may not be known at the time of manufacture or certification. It is for this reason that the emissions are expressed on the basis of brake power as defined in 1.3.13.

**5.1.7** When it is not appropriate to test the engine under the conditions as defined in 5.2.3, e.g., if the engine and transmission form a single integral unit, the engine may only be tested with other auxiliaries fitted. In this case the dynamometer settings shall be determined in accordance with 5.2.3 and 5.9. The auxiliary losses shall not exceed 5% of the maximum observed power. Losses exceeding 5% shall be approved by the Administration involved prior to the test.

**5.1.8** All volumes and volumetric flow rates shall be related to 273 K (0°C) and 101.3 kPa.

**5.1.9** Except as otherwise specified, all results of measurements, test data or calculations required by this chapter shall be recorded in the engine's test report in accordance with 5.10.

**5.1.10** References in this Code to the term "charge air" apply equally to scavenge air.

## 5.2 Test conditions

**5.2.1** *Test condition parameter and test validity for engine family approval*

**5.2.1.1** The absolute temperature $T_a$ of the engine intake air expressed in Kelvin shall be measured, and the dry atmospheric pressure $p_s$, expressed in kPa, shall be measured or calculated as follows:

$$p_s = p_b - 0.01 \cdot R_a \cdot p_a$$

$p_a$ according to formula (10).

**5.2.1.2** For naturally aspirated and mechanically pressure-charged engines the parameter $f_a$ shall be determined according to the following:

$$f_a = \left(\frac{99}{p_s}\right) \cdot \left(\frac{T_a}{298}\right)^{0.7} \tag{1}$$

**5.2.1.3** For turbocharged engines with or without cooling of the intake air the parameter $f_a$ shall be determined according to the following:

$$f_a = \left(\frac{99}{p_s}\right)^{0.7} \cdot \left(\frac{T_a}{298}\right)^{1.5} \tag{2}$$

**5.2.1.4** For a test to be recognized as valid for engine family approval, the parameter $f_a$ shall be such that:

$$0.93 \leq f_a \leq 1.07 \tag{3}$$

**5.2.2** *Engines with charge air cooling*

**5.2.2.1** The temperature of the cooling medium and the charge air temperature shall be recorded.

**5.2.2.2** All engines when equipped as intended for installation on board ships must be capable of operating within the applicable $NO_x$ emission limit of regulation 13 at an ambient seawater temperature of 25°C. This reference temperature shall be considered in accordance with the charge air cooling arrangement applicable to the individual installation as follows:

**.1** Direct seawater cooling to engine charge air coolers. Compliance with the applicable $NO_x$ limit shall be demonstrated with a charge air cooler coolant inlet temperature of 25°C.

**.2** Intermediate freshwater cooling to engine charge air coolers. Compliance with the applicable $NO_x$ limit shall be demonstrated with the charge air cooling system operating with the designed in service coolant inlet temperature regime corresponding to an ambient seawater temperature of 25°C.

*Note:* Demonstration of compliance at a parent engine test for a direct seawater-cooled system, as given by (.1) above, does not demonstrate compliance in accordance with the higher charge air temperature regime inherent with an intermediate freshwater cooling arrangement as required by this section.

**.3** For those installations incorporating no seawater cooling, either direct or indirect, to the charge air coolers, e.g., radiator-cooled freshwater systems, air/air charge air coolers, compliance with the applicable $NO_x$ limit shall be demonstrated with the engine and charge air cooling systems operating as specified by the manufacturer with 25°C air temperature.

**5.2.2.3** Compliance with the applicable $NO_x$ emission limit as defined by regulation 13 shall be demonstrated either by testing or by calculation using the charge air reference temperatures ($T_{SCRef}$) specified and justified by the manufacturer, if applicable.

**5.2.3** *Power*

**5.2.3.1** The basis of specific emissions measurement is uncorrected brake power as defined in 1.3.11 and 1.3.13. The engine shall be submitted with auxiliaries needed for operating the engine (e.g., fan, water pump, etc.). If it is impossible or inappropriate to install the auxiliaries on the test bench, the power absorbed by them shall be determined and subtracted from the measured engine power.

**5.2.3.2** Auxiliaries not necessary for the operation of the engine and that may be mounted on the engine may be removed for the test. See also 5.1.5 and 5.1.6.

**5.2.3.3** Where auxiliaries have not been removed, the power absorbed by them at the test speeds shall be determined in order to calculate the dynamometer settings, except for engines where such auxiliaries form an integral part of the engine (e.g., cooling fans for air-cooled engines).

**5.2.4** *Engine air inlet system*

**5.2.4.1** An engine air intake system or a test shop system shall be used presenting an air intake restriction within ± 300 Pa of the maximum value specified by the manufacturer for a clean air cleaner at the speed of rated power and full load.

**5.2.4.2** If the engine is equipped with an integral air inlet system, it shall be used for testing.

**5.2.5** *Engine exhaust system*

**5.2.5.1** An engine exhaust system or a test shop system shall be used that presents an exhaust backpressure within ± 650 Pa of the maximum value specified by the manufacturer at the speed of rated power and full load. The exhaust system shall conform to the requirements for exhaust gas sampling, as set out in 5.9.3.

**5.2.5.2** If the engine is equipped with an integral exhaust system, it shall be used for testing.

**5.2.5.3** If the engine is equipped with an exhaust after-treatment device, the exhaust pipe shall have the same diameter as found in use for at least 4 pipe diameters upstream to the inlet of the beginning of the expansion section containing the after-treatment device. The distance from the exhaust manifold flange or turbocharger outlet to the exhaust after-treatment device shall be the same as in the on-board configuration or within the distance specifications of the manufacturer. The exhaust backpressure or restriction shall follow the same criteria as above, and may be set with a valve.

**5.2.5.4** Where test-bed installation prevents adjustment to the exhaust gas backpressure as required, the effect on the $NO_x$ emissions shall be demonstrated by the engine builder and, with the approval of the Administration, the emission value duly corrected as necessary.

**5.2.6** *Cooling system*

**5.2.6.1** An engine cooling system with sufficient capacity to maintain the engine at normal operating temperatures prescribed by the manufacturer shall be used.

## 5.3 Test fuel oils

**5.3.1** Fuel oil characteristics may influence the engine exhaust gas emission; in particular, some fuel-bound nitrogen can be converted to $NO_x$ during combustion. Therefore, the characteristics of the fuel oil used for the test are to be determined and recorded. Where a reference fuel oil is used, the reference code or specifications and the analysis of the fuel oil shall be provided.

**5.3.2** The selection of the fuel oil for the test depends on the purpose of the test. If a suitable reference fuel oil is not available, it is recommended to use a DM-grade (distillate) marine fuel specified in ISO 8217:2005, with properties suitable for the engine type. In case a DM-grade fuel oil is not available, an RM-grade (residual) fuel oil according to ISO 8217:2005 shall be used. The fuel oil shall be analysed for its composition of all components necessary for a clear specification and determination of DM or RM grade. The nitrogen content shall also be determined. The fuel oil used during the parent engine test shall be sampled during the test.

**5.3.3** The fuel oil temperature shall be in accordance with the manufacturer's recommendations. The fuel oil temperature shall be measured at the inlet to the fuel injection pump, or as specified by the manufacturer, and the temperature and location of measurement recorded.

**5.3.4** Dual fuel engines using liquid fuel as pilot fuel shall be tested using maximum liquid-to-gas fuel ratio. The liquid fraction of the fuel shall comply with 5.3.1, 5.3.2 and 5.3.3.

## 5.4 Measurement equipment and data to be measured

**5.4.1** The emission of gaseous components by the engine submitted for testing shall be measured by the methods described in appendix III of this Code that describe the recommended analytical systems for the gaseous emissions.

**5.4.2** Other systems or analysers may, subject to the approval of the Administration, be accepted if they yield equivalent results to that of the equipment referenced in 5.4.1. In establishing equivalency it shall be demonstrated that the proposed alternative systems or analysers would, as qualified by using recognized national or international standards, yield equivalent results when used to measure diesel engine exhaust emission concentrations in terms of the requirements referenced in 5.4.1.

**5.4.3** For introduction of a new system the determination of equivalency shall be based upon the calculation of repeatability and reproducibility, as described in ISO 5725-1 and ISO 5725-2, or any other comparable recognized standard.

**5.4.4** This Code does not contain details of flow, pressure, and temperature measuring equipment. Instead, only the accuracy requirements of such equipment necessary for conducting an emissions test are given in 1.3.1 of appendix IV of this Code.

**5.4.5** *Dynamometer specification*

**5.4.5.1** An engine dynamometer with adequate characteristics to perform the appropriate test cycle described in 3.2 shall be used.

**5.4.5.2** The instrumentation for torque and speed measurement shall allow the measurement accuracy of the shaft power within the given limits. Additional calculations may be necessary.

**5.4.5.3** The accuracy of the measuring equipment shall be such that the maximum permissible deviations given in 1.3.1 of appendix IV of this Code are not exceeded.

## 5.5 Determination of exhaust gas flow

**5.5.1** The exhaust gas flow shall be determined by one of the methods specified in 5.5.2, 5.5.3 or 5.5.4.

**5.5.2** *Direct measurement method*

**5.5.2.1** This method involves the direct measurement of the exhaust flow by flow nozzle or equivalent metering system and shall be in accordance with a recognized international standard.

*Note:* Direct gaseous flow measurement is a difficult task. Precautions shall be taken to avoid measurement errors which will result in emission value errors.

**5.5.3** *Air and fuel measurement method*

**5.5.3.1** The method for determining exhaust emission flow using the air and fuel measurement method shall be conducted in accordance with a recognized international standard.

**5.5.3.2** This involves measurement of the air flow and the fuel flow. Air flow-meters and fuel flow-meters with an accuracy defined in 1.3.1 of appendix IV of this Code shall be used.

**5.5.3.3** The exhaust gas flow shall be calculated as follows:

$$q_{mew} = q_{maw} + q_{mf} \tag{4}$$

**5.5.3.4** The air flow-meter shall meet the accuracy specifications of appendix IV of this Code, the $CO_2$ analyser used shall meet the specifications of appendix III of this Code, and the total system shall meet the accuracy specifications for the exhaust gas flow as given in appendix IV of this Code.

**5.5.4** *Fuel flow and carbon balance method*

**5.5.4.1** This involves exhaust mass flow rate calculation from fuel consumption, fuel composition and exhaust gas concentrations using the carbon balance method, as specified in appendix VI of this Code.

## 5.6 Permissible deviations of instruments for engine-related parameters and other essential parameters

**5.6.1** The calibration of all measuring instruments including both the measuring instruments as detailed under appendix IV of this Code and additional measuring instruments required in order to define an engine's $NO_x$ emission performance, for example the measurement of peak cylinder or charge air pressures, shall be traceable to standards recognized by the Administration and shall comply with the requirements as set out in 1.3.1 of appendix IV of this Code.

## 5.7 Analysers for determination of the gaseous components

**5.7.1** The analysers to determine the gaseous emissions shall meet the specifications as set out in appendix III of this Code.

## 5.8 Calibration of the analytical instruments

**5.8.1** Each analyser used for the measurement of an engine's gaseous emissions shall be calibrated in accordance with the requirements of appendix IV of this Code.

## 5.9 Test run

### 5.9.1 *General*

**5.9.1.1** Detailed descriptions of the recommended sampling and analysing systems are contained in 5.9.2 to 5.9.4 and appendix III of this Code. Since various configurations may produce equivalent results, exact conformance with these figures is not required. Additional components, such as instruments, valves, solenoids, pumps and switches, may be used to provide additional information and coordinate the functions of the component systems. Other components that are not needed to maintain the accuracy on some systems may, with the agreement of the Administration, be excluded if their exclusion is based upon good engineering judgement.

**5.9.1.2** The treatment of inlet restriction (naturally aspirated engines) or charge air pressure (turbocharged engines) and exhaust backpressure shall be in accordance with 5.2.4 and 5.2.5, respectively.

**5.9.1.3** In the case of a pressure-charged engine, the inlet restriction conditions shall be taken as the condition with a clean air inlet filter and the pressure charging system working within the bounds as declared, or to be established, for the engine family or engine group to be represented by the parent engine test result.

### 5.9.2 *Main exhaust components: $CO$, $CO_2$, $HC$, $NO_x$ and $O_2$*

**5.9.2.1** An analytical system for the determination of the gaseous emissions in the raw exhaust gas shall be based on the use of analysers given in 5.4.

**5.9.2.2** For the raw exhaust gas, the sample for all components may be taken with one sampling probe or with two sampling probes located in close proximity and internally split to the different analysers. Care must be taken that no condensation of exhaust components (including water and sulphuric acid) occurs at any point of the analytical system.

**5.9.2.3** Specifications and calibration of these analysers shall be as set out in appendices III and IV of this Code, respectively.

**5.9.3** *Sampling for gaseous emissions*

**5.9.3.1** The sampling probes for the gaseous emissions shall be fitted at least 10 pipe diameters after the outlet of the engine, turbocharger, or last after-treatment device, whichever is furthest downstream, but also at least 0.5 m or 3 pipe diameters upstream of the exit of the exhaust gas system, whichever is greater. For a short exhaust system that does not have a location that meets both of these specifications, an alternative sample probe location shall be subject to approval by the Administration.

**5.9.3.2** The exhaust gas temperature shall be at least 190°C at the HC sample probe, and at least 70°C at the sample probes for other measured gas species where they are separate from the HC sample probe.

**5.9.3.3** In the case of a multi-cylinder engine with a branched exhaust manifold, the inlet of the probe shall be located sufficiently far downstream so as to ensure that the sample is representative of the average exhaust emissions from all cylinders. In the case of a multi-cylinder engine having distinct groups of manifolds, it is permissible to acquire a sample from each group individually and calculate an average exhaust emission. Alternatively, it would also be permissible to acquire a sample from a single group to represent the average exhaust emission provided that it can be justified to the Administration that the emissions from other groups are identical. Other methods, subject to the approval of the Administration, that have been shown to correlate with the above methods may be used. For exhaust emission calculation, the total exhaust mass flow shall be used.

**5.9.3.4** The exhaust gas sampling system shall be leakage tested in accordance with section 4 of appendix IV of this Code.

**5.9.3.5** If the composition of the exhaust gas is influenced by any exhaust after-treatment system, the exhaust gas sample shall be taken downstream of that device.

**5.9.3.6** The inlet of the probe shall be located as to avoid ingestion of water that is injected into the exhaust system for the purpose of cooling, tuning or noise reduction.

**5.9.4** *Checking of the analysers*

**5.9.4.1** The emission analysers shall be set at zero and spanned in accordance with section 6 of appendix IV of this Code.

**5.9.5** *Test cycles*

**5.9.5.1** An engine shall be tested in accordance with the test cycles as defined in 3.2. This takes into account the variations in engine application.

**5.9.6** *Test sequence*

**5.9.6.1** After the procedures in 5.9.1 to 5.9.5 have been completed, the test sequence shall be started. The engine shall be operated in each mode, in any order, in accordance with the appropriate test cycles defined in 3.2.

**5.9.6.2** During each mode of the test cycle after the initial transition period, the specified speed shall be held within ± 1% of the rated speed or ± 3 $min^{-1}$, whichever is greater, except for low idle, which shall be within the tolerances declared by the manufacturer. The specified torque shall be held so that the average over the period during which the measurements are being taken is within ± 2% of the rated torque at the engine's rated speed.

**5.9.7** *Analyser response*

**5.9.7.1** When stabilized, the output of the analysers shall be recorded both during the test and during all zero and span response checks, using a data acquisition system or a strip chart recorder. The recording period shall not be less than 10 minutes when analysing exhaust gas or not less than 3 minutes for each zero and span response check. For data acquisition systems, a minimum sampling frequency of 3 per minute shall be used. Measured concentrations of CO, HC and $NO_x$ are to be recorded in terms of, or equivalent to, ppm to at least the nearest whole number. Measured concentrations of $CO_2$ and $O_2$ are to be recorded in terms of, or equivalent to, % to not fewer than two decimal places.

**5.9.8** *Engine conditions*

**5.9.8.1** The engine speed, load and other essential parameters shall be measured at each mode point only after the engine has been stabilized. The exhaust gas flow shall be measured or calculated and recorded.

**5.9.9** *Re-checking the analysers*

**5.9.9.1** After the emission test, the zero and span responses of the analysers shall be re-checked using a zero gas and the same span gas as used prior to the measurements. The test shall be considered acceptable if:

**.1** the difference between the responses to the zero gas before and after the test is less than 2% of the initial span gas concentration; and

**.2** the difference between the responses to the span gas before and after the test is less than 2% of the initial span gas concentration.

**5.9.9.2** Zero- and span-drift correction shall not be applied to the analyser responses recorded in accordance with 5.9.7.

## 5.10 Test report

**5.10.1** For every individual engine or parent engine tested to establish an engine family or engine group, the engine manufacturer shall prepare a test report that shall contain the necessary data to fully define the engine performance and enable calculation of the gaseous emissions including the data as set out in section 1 of appendix V of this Code. The original of the test report shall be maintained on file with the engine manufacturer and a certified true copy shall be maintained on file by the Administration.

## 5.11 Data evaluation for gaseous emissions

**5.11.1** For the evaluation of the gaseous emissions, the data recorded for at least the last 60 seconds of each mode shall be averaged, and the concentrations of CO, $CO_2$, HC, $NO_x$, and $O_2$ during each mode shall be determined from the averaged recorded data and the corresponding zero and span check data. The averaged results shall be given in terms of % to not fewer than two decimal places for $CO_2$ and $O_2$ species and in terms of ppm to at least the nearest whole number for CO, HC and $NO_x$ species.

## 5.12 Calculation of the gaseous emissions

**5.12.1** The final results for the test report shall be determined by following the steps in 5.12.2 to 5.12.6.

### 5.12.2 *Determination of the exhaust gas flow*

**5.12.2.1** The exhaust gas flow rate ($q_{mew}$) shall be determined for each mode in accordance with one of the methods described in 5.5.2 to 5.5.4.

### 5.12.3 *Dry/wet correction*

**5.12.3.1** If the emissions are not measured on a wet basis, the measured concentration shall be converted to a wet basis according to the following formulae:

$$c_w = k_w \cdot c_d \tag{5}$$

**5.12.3.2** For the raw exhaust gas:

**.1** Complete combustion where exhaust gas flow is to be determined in accordance with direct measurement method in 5.5.2 or air and fuel measurement method in 5.5.3 – either of the following formulae shall be used:

$$k_{wr1} = \left(1 - \frac{1.2442 \cdot H_a + 111.19 \cdot w_{ALF} \cdot \frac{q_{mf}}{q_{mad}}}{773.4 + 1.2442 \cdot H_a + \frac{q_{mf}}{q_{mad}} \cdot f_{fw} \cdot 1000}\right) \cdot 1.008 \tag{6}$$

or

$$k_{wr1} = \left(1 - \frac{1.2442 \cdot H_a + 111.19 \cdot w_{ALF} \cdot \frac{q_{mf}}{q_{mad}}}{773.4 + 1.2442 \cdot H_a + \frac{q_{mf}}{q_{mad}} \cdot f_{fw} \cdot 1000}\right) \Big/ \left(1 - \frac{p_r}{p_b}\right) \tag{7}$$

with:

$$f_{fw} = 0.055594 \cdot w_{ALF} + 0.0080021 \cdot w_{DEL} + 0.0070046 \cdot w_{EPS} \tag{8}$$

$H_a$ is the absolute humidity of intake air, in g water per kg dry air

*Note:* $H_a$ may be derived from relative humidity measurement, dew point measurement, vapour pressure measurement or dry/wet bulb measurement using the generally accepted formulae.

$$H_a = 6.22 \cdot p_a \cdot R_a / (p_b - 0.01 \cdot R_a \cdot p_a) \tag{9}$$

where:

$p_a$ = saturation vapour pressure of the intake air, kPa

$$p_a = (4.856884 + 0.2660089 \cdot t_a + 0.01688919 \cdot t_a^2 - 7.477123 \cdot 10^{-5} \cdot t_a^3 + 8.10525 \cdot 10^{-6}\ t_a^4 - 3.115221 \cdot 10^{-8} \cdot t_a^5) \cdot (101.32 / 760) \qquad (10)$$

with:

$t_a$ = temperature of the intake air, °C; $t_a = T_a - 273.15$

$p_b$ = total barometric pressure, kPa

$p_r$ = water vapour pressure after cooling bath of the analysis system, kPa

$p_r$ = 0.76 kPa for cooling bath temperature 3°C

**.2** Incomplete combustion, CO more than 100 ppm or HC more than 100 ppmC at one or more mode points, where exhaust gas flow is determined in accordance with direct measurement method 5.5.2, air and fuel measurement method 5.5.3 and in all cases where the carbon balance method 5.5.4 is used – the following equation shall be used:

*Note:* The unit for the CO and $CO_2$ concentrations in (11) and (13) is %.

$$k_{wr2} = \frac{1}{1+\alpha \cdot 0.005 \cdot (c_{CO2d}+c_{COd}) - 0.01 \cdot c_{H2d} + k_{w2} - \frac{p_r}{p_b}} \qquad (11)$$

with:

$$\alpha = 11.9164 \cdot \frac{w_{ALF}}{w_{BET}} \qquad (12)$$

$$c_{H2d} = \frac{0.5 \cdot \alpha \cdot c_{COd} \cdot (c_{COd} + c_{CO2d})}{c_{COd} + 3 \cdot c_{CO2d}} \qquad (13)$$

$$k_{w2} = \frac{1.608 \cdot H_a}{1000 + (1.608 \cdot H_a)} \qquad (14)$$

**5.12.3.3** For the intake air:

$$k_{wa} = 1 - k_{w2} \qquad (15)$$

### 5.12.4 *$NO_x$ correction for humidity and temperature*

**5.12.4.1** As the $NO_x$ emission depends on ambient air conditions, the $NO_x$ concentration shall be corrected for ambient air temperature and humidity with the factors in accordance with 5.12.4.5 or 5.12.4.6 as applicable.

**5.12.4.2** Other reference values for humidity instead of 10.71 g/kg at the reference temperature of 25°C shall not be used.

**5.12.4.3** Other correction formulae may be used if they can be justified, validated and are approved by the Administration.

**5.12.4.4** Water or steam injected into the charge air (air humidification) is considered an emission control device and shall therefore not be taken into account for humidity correction. Water that condensates in the charge cooler will change the humidity of the charge air and therefore shall be taken into account for humidity correction.

**5.12.4.5** For compression ignition engines:

$$k_{hd} = \frac{1}{1-0.0182\cdot(H_a-10.71)+0.0045\cdot(T_a-298)} \qquad (16)$$

where:

$T_a$ = the temperature of the air at the inlet to the air filter in K;

$H_a$ = the humidity of the intake air at the inlet to the air filter in g water per kg dry air.

**5.12.4.6** For compression ignition engines with intermediate air cooler the following alternative equation shall be used:

$$k_{hd} = \frac{1}{1-0.012\cdot(H_a-10.71)-0.00275\cdot(T_a-298)+0.00285\cdot(T_{SC}-T_{SCRef})} \qquad (17)$$

where:

$T_{SC}$ is the temperature of the charge air;

$T_{SCRef}$ is the temperature of the charge air at each mode point corresponding to a seawater temperature of 25°C as specified in 5.2.2. $T_{SCRef}$ is to be specified by the manufacturer.

To take the humidity in the charge air into account, the following consideration is added:

$H_{SC}$ = humidity of the charge air, g water per kg dry air in which:
$H_{SC} = 6.22 \cdot p_{SC} \cdot 100 / (p_C - p_{SC})$

where:

$p_{SC}$ = saturation vapour pressure of the charge air, kPa
$p_C$ = charge air pressure, kPa

However if $H_a \geq H_{SC}$, then $H_{SC}$ shall be used in place of $H_a$ in formula (17).

### 5.12.5 *Calculation of the emission mass flow rates*

**5.12.5.1** The emission mass flow rate of the respective component in the raw exhaust gas for each mode shall be calculated in accordance with 5.12.5.2 from the measured concentration as obtained in accordance with 5.11.1, the applicable $u_{gas}$ value from table 5 and the exhaust gas mass flow rate in accordance with 5.5.

*Table 5* – Coefficient $u_{gas}$ and fuel-specific parameters for raw exhaust gas

| **Gas** | | **$NO_x$** | **CO** | **HC** | **$CO_2$** | **$O_2$** |
|---|---|---|---|---|---|---|
| $\rho_{gas}$ kg/m$^3$ | | 2.053 | 1.250 | * | 1.9636 | 1.4277 |
| | $\rho_e$† | Coefficient $u_{gas}$‡ | | | | |
| Fuel oil | 1.2943 | 0.001586 | 0.000966 | 0.000479 | 0.001517 | 0.001103 |

* Depending on fuel.

† $\rho_e$ is the nominal density of the exhaust gas.

‡ At $\lambda = 2$, wet air, 273 K, 101.3 kPa.

Values for $u$ given in table 5 are based on ideal gas properties.

**5.12.5.2** The following formulae shall be applied:

$$q_{mgas} = u_{gas} \cdot c_{gas} \cdot q_{mew} \cdot k_{hd} \text{ (for NO}_x\text{)} \tag{18}$$

$$q_{mgas} = u_{gas} \cdot c_{gas} \cdot q_{mew} \cdot \text{ (for other gases)} \tag{18a}$$

where:

$q_{mgas}$ = emission mass flow rate of individual gas, g/h

$u_{gas}$ = ratio between density of exhaust component and density of exhaust gas, see table 5

$c_{gas}$ = concentration of the respective component in the raw exhaust gas, ppm, wet

$q_{mew}$ = exhaust mass flow, kg/h, wet

$k_{hd}$ = $NO_x$ humidity correction factor

*Note:* In the case of $CO_2$ and $O_2$ measurement, the concentration will normally be reported in terms of %. With regard to the application of formula 18a, these concentrations will need to be expressed in ppm. 1.0% = 10000 ppm.

**5.12.5.3** For the calculation of $NO_x$, the humidity correction factor $k_{hd}$ as determined according to 5.12.4 shall be used.

**5.12.5.4** The measured concentration shall be converted to a wet basis according to 5.12.3 if not already measured on a wet basis.

**5.12.6** *Calculation of the specific emission*

**5.12.6.1** The emission shall be calculated for all individual components in accordance with the following:

$$1. \quad gas_x = \frac{\sum_{i=1}^{i=n} (q_{mgas_i} \cdot W_{F_i})}{\sum_{i=1}^{i=n} (P_i \cdot W_{F_i})} \tag{19}$$

where:

$$2. \quad P = P_m + P_{aux} \tag{20}$$

and

$q_{mgas}$ is the mass flow of individual gas;

$P_m$ is the measured power of the individual mode;

$P_{aux}$ is the power of the auxiliaries fitted to the engine of the individual mode.

**5.12.6.2** The weighting factors and the number of modes (*n*) used in the above calculation shall be according to the provisions of 3.2.

**5.12.6.3** The resulting average weighted $NO_x$ emission value for the engine as determined by formula (19) shall then be compared to the applicable emission limit given in regulation 13 to determine if the engine is in compliance.

# Chapter 6

## *Procedures for demonstrating compliance with $NO_x$ emission limits on board*

### 6.1 General

**6.1.1** After installation of a pre-certificated engine on board a ship, every marine diesel engine shall have an on-board verification survey conducted as specified in 2.1.1.2 to 2.1.1.4 to verify that the engine continues to comply with the applicable $NO_x$ emission limit contained in regulation 13. Such verification of compliance shall be determined by using one of the following methods:

- **.1** engine parameter check method in accordance with 6.2 to verify that an engine's component, settings and operating values have not deviated from the specifications in the engine's technical file;
- **.2** simplified measurement method in accordance with 6.3; or
- **.3** direct measurement and monitoring method in accordance with 6.4.

### 6.2 Engine parameter check method

**6.2.1** *General*

**6.2.1.1** Engines that meet the following conditions shall be eligible for an engine parameter check method:

- **.1** engines that have received a pre-certificate (EIAPP Certificate) on the test bed and those that received a certificate (EIAPP Certificate) following an initial certification survey in accordance with 2.2.4; and
- **.2** engines that have undergone modifications or adjustments to the designated engine components and adjustable features since they were last surveyed.

**6.2.1.2** When a diesel engine is designed to run within the applicable $NO_x$ emission limit, it is most likely that within the marine life of the engine, the $NO_x$ emission limit may be adhered to. The applicable $NO_x$ emission limit may, however, be contravened by adjustments or modification to the engine. Therefore, an engine parameter check method shall be used to verify whether the engine is still within the applicable $NO_x$ emission limit.

**6.2.1.3** Engine component checks, including checks of settings and an engine's operating values, are intended to provide an easy means of deducing the emissions performance of the engine for the purpose of verification that an engine with no, or minor, adjustments or modifications complies with the applicable $NO_x$ emission limit. Where the measurement of some operating values is required, the calibration of the equipment used for those measurements shall be in accordance with the requirements of appendix IV of this Code.

**6.2.1.4** The purpose of such checks is to provide a ready means of determining that an engine is correctly adjusted in accordance with the manufacturer's specification and remains in a condition of adjustment consistent with the initial certification by the Administration as being in compliance with regulation 13 as applicable.

**6.2.1.5** If an electronic engine management system is employed, this shall be evaluated against the original settings to ensure that appropriate parameters are operating within "as-built" limits.

**6.2.1.6** For the purpose of assessing compliance with regulation 13, it is not always necessary to measure the $NO_x$ emissions to know that an engine not equipped with an after-treatment device is likely to comply with the applicable $NO_x$ emission limit. It may be sufficient to know that the present state of the engine corresponds to the specified components, calibration or parameter adjustment state at the time of initial certification. If the results of an engine parameter check method indicate the likelihood that the engine complies with the applicable $NO_x$ emission limit, the engine may be re-certified without direct $NO_x$ measurement.

**6.2.1.7** For an engine equipped with an $NO_x$-reducing device, it will be necessary to check the operation of the device as part of the engine parameter check method.

**6.2.2** *Documentation for an engine parameter check method*

**6.2.2.1** Every marine diesel engine shall have a technical file as required in 2.3.4 that identifies the engine's components, settings or operating values that influence exhaust emissions and must be checked to ensure compliance.

**6.2.2.2** An engine's technical file shall contain all applicable information, relevant to the $NO_x$ emission performance of the engine, on the designated engine's components, adjustable features and parameters at the time of the engine's pre-certification or on-board certification, whichever occurred first.

**6.2.2.3** Dependent on the specific design of the particular engine, different on-board $NO_x$-influencing modifications and adjustments are possible and usual. These include the engine parameters as follows:

- **.1** injection timing,
- **.2** injection nozzle,
- **.3** injection pump,
- **.4** fuel cam,
- **.5** injection pressure for common rail systems,
- **.6** combustion chamber,
- **.7** compression ratio,
- **.8** turbocharger type and build,
- **.9** charge air cooler, charge air pre-heater,
- **.10** valve timing,
- **.11** $NO_x$ abatement equipment "water injection",
- **.12** $NO_x$ abatement equipment "emulsified fuel" (fuel water emulsion),
- **.13** $NO_x$ abatement equipment "exhaust gas recirculation",
- **.14** $NO_x$ abatement equipment "selective catalytic reduction", or
- **.15** other parameter(s) specified by the Administration.

**6.2.2.4** The actual technical file of an engine may, based on the recommendations of the applicant for engine certification and the approval of the Administration, include fewer components and/or parameters than discussed in section 6.2.2.3, depending on the particular engine and the specific design.

**6.2.2.5** For some parameters, different survey possibilities exist. As approved by the Administration, the shipowner, supported by the applicant for engine certification, may choose what method is applicable. Any one of, or a combination of, the methods listed in the checklist for the engine parameter check method given in appendix VII of this Code may be sufficient to show compliance.

**6.2.2.6** Technical documentation in respect of engine component modification for inclusion in an engine's technical file shall include details of that modification and its influence on $NO_x$ emissions, and it shall be supplied at the time when the modification is carried out. Test-bed data obtained from a later engine that is within the applicable range of the engine group concept may be accepted.

**6.2.2.7** The shipowner or person responsible for a ship equipped with a marine diesel engine required to undergo an engine parameter check method shall maintain on board the following documentation in relation to the on-board $NO_x$ verification procedures:

**.1** a record book of engine parameters for recording all changes, including like-for-like replacements, and adjustments within the approved ranges made relative to an engine's components and settings;

**.2** an engine parameter list of an engine's designated components and settings and/or the documentation of an engine's load-dependent operating values submitted by an applicant for engine certification and approved by the Administration; and

**.3** technical documentation of an engine component modification when such a modification is made to any of the engine's designated engine components.

**6.2.2.8** Descriptions of any changes affecting the designated engine parameters, including adjustments, parts replacements and modifications to engine parts, shall be recorded chronologically in the record book of engine parameters. These descriptions shall be supplemented with any other applicable data used for the assessment of the engine's $NO_x$ emissions.

**6.2.3** *Procedures for an engine parameter check method*

**6.2.3.1** An engine parameter check method shall be carried out using the two procedures as follows:

**.1** a documentation inspection of engine parameter(s) shall be carried out in addition to other inspections and include inspection of the record book of engine parameters and verification that engine parameters are within the allowable range specified in the engine's technical file; and

**.2** an actual inspection of engine components and adjustable features shall be carried out as necessary. It shall then be verified, also referring to the results of the documentation inspection, that the engine's adjustable features are within the allowable range specified in the engine's technical file.

**6.2.3.2** The surveyor shall have the option of checking one or all of the identified components, settings or operating values to ensure that the engine with no, or minor, adjustments or modifications complies with the applicable $NO_x$ emission limit and that only components of the approved specification, as given by 2.4.1.7, are being used. Where adjustments and/or modifications in a specification are referenced in the technical file, they must fall within the range recommended by the applicant for engine certification and approved by the Administration.

## 6.3 Simplified measurement method

### 6.3.1 *General*

**6.3.1.1** The following simplified test and measurement procedure specified in this section shall be applied only for on-board confirmation tests and renewal, annual and intermediate surveys when required. Every first engine testing on a test bed shall be carried out in accordance with the procedure specified in chapter 5. Corrections for ambient air humidity and temperature in accordance with 5.12.4 are essential, as ships are sailing in cold/hot and dry/humid climates, which may cause a difference in $NO_x$ emissions.

**6.3.1.2** To gain meaningful results for on-board confirmation tests and on-board renewal, annual and intermediate surveys, as an absolute minimum, the gaseous emission concentrations of $NO_x$ and $CO_2$ shall be measured in accordance with the appropriate test cycle. The weighting factors ($W_F$) and the number of modes ($n$) used in the calculation shall be in accordance with 3.2.

**6.3.1.3** The engine torque and engine speed shall be measured but, to simplify the procedure, the permissible deviations of instruments (see 6.3.7) for measurement of engine-related parameters for on-board verification purposes are different than those permissible deviations allowed under the test-bed testing method. If it is difficult to measure the torque directly, the brake power may be estimated by any other means recommended by the applicant for engine certification and approved by the Administration.

**6.3.1.4** In practical cases, it is often impossible to measure the fuel oil consumption once an engine has been installed on board a ship. To simplify the procedure on board, the results of the measurement of the fuel oil consumption from an engine's pre-certification test-bed testing may be accepted. In such cases, especially concerning residual fuel oil operation (RM-grade fuel oil according to ISO 8217:2005), an estimation with a corresponding estimated error shall be made. Since the fuel oil flow rate used in the calculation ($q_{mf}$) must relate to the fuel oil composition determined in respect of the fuel sample drawn during the test, the measurement of $q_{mf}$ from the test-bed testing shall be corrected for any difference in net calorific values between the test bed and test fuel oils. The consequences of such an error on the final emissions shall be calculated and reported with the results of the emission measurement.

**6.3.1.5** Except as otherwise specified, all results of measurements, test data or calculations required by this chapter shall be recorded in the engine's test report in accordance with 5.10.

**6.3.2** *Engine parameters to be measured and recorded*

**6.3.2.1** Table 6 lists the engine parameters that shall be measured and recorded during on-board verification procedures.

*Table 6* – Engine parameters to be measured and recorded

| Symbol | Term | Unit |
|---|---|---|
| $H_a$ | Absolute humidity (mass of engine intake air water content related to mass of dry air) | g/kg |
| $n_{d,i}$ | Engine speed (at the $i^{th}$ mode during the cycle) | $min^{-1}$ |
| $n_{turb,i}$ | Turbocharger speed (if applicable) (at the $i^{th}$ mode during the cycle) | $min^{-1}$ |
| $p_b$ | Total barometric pressure (in ISO 3046-1: 1995: $p_x$ = Px = site ambient total pressure) | kPa |
| $p_{C,i}$ | Charge air pressure after the charge air cooler (at the $i^{th}$ mode during the cycle) | kPa |
| $P_i$ | Brake power (at the $i^{th}$ mode during the cycle) | kW |

| Symbol | Term | Unit |
|---|---|---|
| $q_{mf,i}$ | Fuel oil flow (at the $i^{th}$ mode during the cycle) | kg/h |
| $s_i$ | Fuel rack position (of each cylinder, if applicable) (at the $i^{th}$ mode during the cycle) | |
| $T_a$ | Intake air temperature at air inlet (in ISO 3046-1:1995: $T_x$ = TTx = site ambient thermodynamic air temperature) | K |
| $T_{SC,i}$ | Charge air temperature after the charge air cooler (if applicable) (at the $i^{th}$ mode during the cycle) | K |
| $T_{caclin}$ | Charge air cooler, coolant inlet temperature | °C |
| $T_{caclout}$ | Charge air cooler, coolant outlet temperature | °C |
| $T_{Exh,i}$ | Exhaust gas temperature at the sampling point (at the $i^{th}$ mode during the cycle) | °C |
| $T_{Fuel}$ | Fuel oil temperature before the engine | °C |
| $T_{Sea}$ | Seawater temperature | °C |

**6.3.3** *Brake power*

**6.3.3.1** The point regarding the ability to obtain the required data during on-board $NO_x$ testing is particularly relevant to brake power. Although the case of directly coupled gearboxes is considered in chapter 5 (5.1.7), an engine, as may be presented on board, could, in many applications, be arranged such that the measurements of torque (as obtained from a specially installed strain gauge) may not be possible due to the absence of a clear shaft. Principal in this context would be generators, but engines may also be coupled to pumps, hydraulic units, compressors, etc.

**6.3.3.2** The engines driving the machinery given in 6.3.3.1 would typically have been tested against a water brake at the manufacture stage prior to the permanent connection of the power-consuming unit when installed on board. For generators it should not pose a problem to use voltage and amperage measurements together with a manufacturer's declared generator efficiency. For propeller-law-governed equipment, a declared speed power curve may be applied together with ensured capability to measure engine speed, either from the free end or by ratio of, for example, the camshaft speed.

**6.3.4** *Test fuel oils*

**6.3.4.1** Generally all emission measurements shall be carried out with the engine running on marine diesel fuel oil of an ISO 8217:2005, DM grade.

**6.3.4.2** To avoid an unacceptable burden to the shipowner, the measurements for confirmation tests or re-surveys may, based on the recommendation of the applicant for engine certification and the approval of the Administration, be allowed with an engine running on residual fuel oil of an ISO 8217:2005, RM grade. In such a case the fuel-bound nitrogen and the ignition quality of the fuel oil may have an influence on the $NO_x$ emissions of the engine.

**6.3.5** *Sampling for gaseous emissions*

**6.3.5.1** The general requirements described in 5.9.3 shall be also applied for on-board measurements.

**6.3.5.2** The installation on board of all engines shall be such that these tests may be performed safely and with minimal interference to the engine. Adequate arrangements for the sampling of the exhaust gas and the ability to obtain the required data shall be provided on board a ship. The uptakes of all engines shall be fitted with an accessible standard sampling point. An example of a sample point connection flange is given in section 5 of appendix VIII of this Code.

**6.3.6** *Measurement equipment and data to be measured*

**6.3.6.1** The emission of gaseous pollutants shall be measured by the methods described in chapter 5.

**6.3.7** *Permissible deviation of instruments for engine-related parameters and other essential parameters*

**6.3.7.1** Tables 3 and 4 contained in section 1.3 of appendix IV of this Code list the permissible deviation of instruments to be used in the measurement of engine-related parameters and other essential parameters during on-board verification procedures.

**6.3.8** *Determination of the gaseous components*

**6.3.8.1** The analytical measuring equipment and the methods described in chapter 5 shall be applied.

**6.3.9** *Test cycles*

**6.3.9.1** Test cycles used on board shall conform to the applicable test cycles specified in 3.2.

**6.3.9.2** Engine operation on board under a test cycle specified in 3.2 may not always be possible, but the test procedure shall, based on the recommendation of the engine manufacturer and approval by the Administration, be as close as possible to the procedure defined in 3.2. Therefore, values measured in this case may not be directly comparable with test-bed results because measured values are very much dependent on the test cycles.

**6.3.9.3** If the number of measuring points on board is different than those on the test bed, the measuring points and the weighting factors shall be in accordance with the recommendations of the applicant for engine certification and approved by the Administration, taking into account the provisions of 6.4.6.

**6.3.10** *Calculation of gaseous emissions*

**6.3.10.1** The calculation procedure specified in chapter 5 shall be applied, taking into account the special requirements of this simplified measurement procedure.

**6.3.11** *Allowances*

**6.3.11.1** Due to the possible deviations when applying the simplified measurement procedures of this chapter on board a ship, an allowance of 10% of the applicable limit value may be accepted for confirmation tests and renewal, annual and intermediate surveys only.

**6.3.11.2** The $NO_x$ emission of an engine may vary depending on the ignition quality of the fuel oil and the fuel-bound nitrogen. If there is insufficient information available on the influence of the ignition quality on the $NO_x$ formation during the combustion process and the fuel-bound nitrogen conversion rate also depends on the engine efficiency, an allowance of 10% may be granted for an on-board test run carried out on an RM-grade fuel oil (ISO 8217:2005), except that there will be no allowance for the pre-certification test on board. The fuel oil used shall be analysed for its composition of carbon, hydrogen, nitrogen, sulphur and, to the extent given in ISO 8217:2005, any additional components necessary for a clear specification of the fuel oil.

**6.3.11.3** In no case shall the total granted allowance for both the simplification of measurements on board and the use of residual fuel oil of an ISO 8217:2005, RM-grade, fuel oil exceed 15% of the applicable limit value.

## 6.4 Direct measurement and monitoring method

### 6.4.1 *General*

**6.4.1.1** The following direct measurement and monitoring procedure may be applied for on-board verification at renewal, annual and intermediate surveys.

**6.4.1.2** Due attention is to be given to the safety implications related to the handling and proximity of exhaust gases, the measurement equipment and the storage and use of cylindered pure and calibration gases. Sampling positions and access staging shall be such that this monitoring may be performed safely and will not interfere with the engine.

### 6.4.2 *Emission species measurement*

**6.4.2.1** On-board $NO_x$ monitoring includes, as an absolute minimum, the measurement of gaseous emission concentrations of $NO_x$ (as $NO + NO_2$).

**6.4.2.2** If exhaust gas mass flow is to be determined in accordance with the carbon balance method in accordance with appendix VI of this Code, then $CO_2$ shall also be measured. Additionally CO, HC and $O_2$ may be measured.

### 6.4.3 *Engine performance measurements*

**6.4.3.1** Table 7 lists the engine performance parameters that shall be measured, or calculated, and recorded at each mode point during on-board $NO_x$ monitoring.

**6.4.3.2** Other engine settings necessary to define engine operating conditions, e.g., waste gate, charge air bypass, turbocharger status, shall be determined and recorded.

**6.4.3.3** The settings and operating conditions of any $NO_x$-reducing devices shall be determined and recorded.

*Table* 7 – Engine performance parameters to be measured and recorded

| Symbol | Term | Unit |
|---|---|---|
| $n_d$ | Engine speed | $min^{-1}$ |
| $p_C$ | Charge air pressure at receiver | kPa |
| $P$ | Brake power (as specified below) | kW |
| $P_{aux}$ | Auxiliary power (if relevant) | kW |
| $T_{sc}$ | Charge air temperature at receiver (if applicable) | K |
| $T_{caclin}$ | Charge air cooler, coolant inlet temperature (if applicable) | °C |
| $T_{caclout}$ | Charge air cooler, coolant outlet temperature (if applicable) | °C |
| $T_{Sea}$ | Seawater temperature (if applicable) | °C |
| $q_{mf}$ | Fuel oil flow (as specified below) | kg/h |

**6.4.3.4** If it is difficult to measure power directly, uncorrected brake power may be estimated by any other means as approved by the Administration. Possible methods to determine brake power include, but are not limited to:

**.1** indirect measurement in accordance with 6.3.3; or

**.2** by estimation from nomographs.

**6.4.3.5** The fuel oil flow (actual consumption rate) shall be determined by:

**.1** direct measurement; or

**.2** test-bed data in accordance with 6.3.1.4

**6.4.4** *Ambient condition measurements*

**6.4.4.1** Table 8 lists the ambient condition parameters that shall be measured, or calculated, and recorded at each mode point during on-board $NO_x$ monitoring.

**6.4.5** *Engine performance and ambient condition monitoring equipment*

**6.4.5.1** The engine performance and ambient condition monitoring equipment shall be installed and maintained in accordance with manufacturers' recommendations such that requirements of section 1.3 and tables 3 and 4 of appendix IV of this Code are met in respect of the permissible deviations.

*Table 8* – Ambient condition parameters to be measured and recorded

| Symbol | Term | Unit |
|---|---|---|
| $H_a$ | Absolute humidity (mass of engine intake air water content related to mass of dry air) | g/kg |
| $p_b$ | Total barometric pressure (in ISO 3046-1: 1995: $p_x$ = Px = site ambient total pressure) | kPa |
| $T_a$ | Temperature at air inlet (in ISO 3046-1: 1995: $T_x$ = TTx = site ambient thermo-dynamic air temperature) | K |

**6.4.6** *Test cycles*

**6.4.6.1** Engine operation on board under a specified test cycle may not always be possible, but the test procedure, as approved by the Administration, shall be as close as possible to the procedure defined in 3.2. Therefore, values measured in this case may not be directly comparable with test-bed results because measured values are very much dependent on the test cycle.

**6.4.6.2** In the case of the E3 test cycle, if the actual propeller curve differs from the E3 curve, the load point used shall be set using the engine speed, or the corresponding mean effective pressure (MEP) or mean indicated pressure (MIP), given for the relevant mode of that cycle.

**6.4.6.3** Where the number of measuring points on board is different from those on the test bed, the number of measuring points and the associated revised weighting factors shall be approved by the Administration.

**6.4.6.4** Further to 6.4.6.3, where the E2, E3 or D2 test cycles are applied, a minimum of load points shall be used of which the combined nominal weighting factor, as given in 3.2, is greater than 0.5.

**6.4.6.5** Further to 6.4.6.3, where the C1 test cycle is applied, a minimum of one load point shall be used from each of the rated, intermediate and idle speed sections. If the number of measuring points on board is different from those on the test bed, the nominal weighting factors at each load point shall be increased proportionally in order to sum to unity (1.0).

**6.4.6.6** With regard to the application of 6.4.6.3, guidance in respect of the selection of load points and revised weighting factors is given in section 6 of appendix VIII of this Code.

**6.4.6.7** The actual load points used to demonstrate compliance shall be within ± 5% of the rated power at the modal point except in the case of 100% load, where the range shall be +0 to −10%. For example, at the 75% load point the acceptable range shall be 70%–80% of rated power.

**6.4.6.8** At each selected load point, except idle, and after the initial transition period (if applicable), the engine power shall be maintained at the load set point within a 5% coefficient of variance (% C.O.V.) over a 10-minute interval. A worked example of the coefficient of variance calculation is given in section 7 of appendix VIII of this Code.

**6.4.6.9** Regarding the C1 test cycle, the idle speed tolerance shall be declared, subject to the approval of the Administration.

**6.4.7** *Test condition parameter*

**6.4.7.1** The test condition parameter specified in 5.2.1 shall not apply to on-board $NO_x$ monitoring. Data under any prevailing ambient condition shall be acceptable.

**6.4.8** *Analyser in-service performance*

**6.4.8.1** Analysing equipment shall be operated in accordance with manufacturer's recommendations.

**6.4.8.2** Prior to measurement, zero and span values shall be checked and the analysers shall be adjusted as necessary.

**6.4.8.3** After measurement, analyser zero and span values shall be verified as being within that permitted by 5.9.9.

**6.4.9** *Data for emission calculation*

**6.4.9.1** The output of the analysers shall be recorded both during the test and during all response checks (zero and span). These data shall be recorded on a strip chart recorder or other types of data recording devices. Data recording precision shall be in accordance with 5.9.7.1.

**6.4.9.2** For the evaluation of the gaseous emissions, a 1-Hertz minimum chart reading of a stable 10-minute sampling interval of each load point shall be averaged. The average concentrations of $NO_x$, and, if required, $CO_2$, and, optionally, CO, HC and $O_2$, shall be determined from the averaged chart readings and the corresponding calibration data.

**6.4.9.3** As a minimum, emission concentrations, engine performance and ambient condition data shall be recorded over the aforementioned 10-minute period.

**6.4.10** *Exhaust gas flow rate*

**6.4.10.1** Exhaust gas flow rate shall be determined:

**.1** in accordance with 5.5.2 or 5.5.3; or

**.2** in accordance with 5.5.4 and appendix VI of this Code, with not-measured species set to zero and $c_{CO2d}$ set to 0.03%.

**6.4.11** *Fuel oil composition*

**6.4.11.1** Fuel oil composition, to calculate gas mass flow wet, $q_{mf}$, shall be provided by one of the following:

**.1** fuel oil composition, carbon, hydrogen, nitrogen and oxygen, by analysis (default oxygen value may be adopted); or

**.2** default values as given in table 9.

*Table 9* – Default fuel oil parameters

| | Carbon | Hydrogen | Nitrogen | Oxygen |
|---|---|---|---|---|
| | $w_{BET}$ | $w_{ALF}$ | $w_{DEL}$ | $w_{EPS}$ |
| Distillate fuel oil (ISO 8217:2005, DM grade) | 86.2% | 13.6% | 0.0% | 0.0% |
| Residual fuel oil (ISO 8217:2005, RM grade) | 86.1% | 10.9% | 0.4% | 0.0% |

**6.4.12** *Dry/wet correction*

**6.4.12.1** If not already measured on a wet basis, the gaseous emissions concentrations shall be converted to a wet basis according to:

**.1** direct measurement of the water component; or

**.2** dry/wet correction calculated in accordance with 5.12.3.

**6.4.13** *$NO_x$ correction for humidity and temperature*

**6.4.13.1** $NO_x$ correction for humidity and temperature shall be in accordance with 5.12.4. The reference charge air temperature ($T_{SCRef}$) shall be stated and approved by the Administration. The $T_{SCRef}$ values are to be referenced to 25°C seawater temperature and in the application of the $T_{SCRef}$ value due allowance shall be made for the actual seawater temperature.

**6.4.14** *Calculation of emission flow rates and specific emissions*

**6.4.14.1** The calculation of emission flow rates and specific emissions shall be in accordance with 5.12.5 and 5.12.6.

**6.4.15** *Limit value and allowances*

**6.4.15.1** In the case of the application of 6.4.6.3 the emission value obtained shall, subject to the approval of the Administration, be corrected as follows:

$$\text{Corrected gas}_x = \text{gas}_x \cdot 0.9 \tag{21}$$

**6.4.15.2** The emission value, $\text{gas}_x$ or corrected $\text{gas}_x$ as appropriate, shall be compared to the applicable $NO_x$ emission limit value as given in regulation 13 together with the allowance values as given in 6.3.11.1, 6.3.11.2 and 6.3.11.3 in order to verify that an engine continues to comply with the requirements of regulation 13.

**6.4.16** *Data for demonstrating compliance*

**6.4.16.1** Compliance is required to be demonstrated at renewal, annual and intermediate surveys or following a substantial modification as per 1.3.2. In accordance with 2.4.5, data are required to be current; that is, within 30 days. Data are required to be retained on board for at least three months. These time periods shall be taken to be when the ship is in operation. Data within that 30-day period either may be collected as a single test sequence across the required load points or may be obtained on two or more separate occasions when the engine load corresponds to that required by 6.4.6.

**6.4.17** *Form of approval*

**6.4.17.1** The direct measurement and monitoring method shall be documented in an on-board monitoring manual. The on-board monitoring manual shall be submitted to the Administration for approval. The approval reference of that on-board monitoring manual shall be entered under section 3 of the supplement to the EIAPP Certificate. The Administration may issue a new EIAPP Certificate, with the details in section 3 of the supplement duly amended, if the method is approved after the issue of the first EIAPP Certificate, i.e., following the pre-certification survey.

**6.4.18** *Survey of equipment and method*

**6.4.18.1** The survey of the direct measurement and monitoring method shall take into account, but is not limited to:

- **.1** the data obtained and developed from the required measurements; and
- **.2** the means by which those data have been obtained, taking into account the information given in the on-board monitoring manual, as required by 6.4.14.

# Chapter 7

## *Certification of an existing engine*

**7.1** Where an existing engine is to comply with regulation 13.7, then the entity responsible for obtaining emissions certification shall apply to the approving Administration for certification.

**7.2** Where an application for approved method approval includes gaseous emission measurements and calculations, those are to be in accordance with chapter 5.

**7.3** Emission and performance data obtained from one engine may be shown to apply to a range of engines.

**7.4** The approved method for achieving compliance with regulation 13.7 shall include a copy of the approved method file that is required to accompany the engine throughout its life on board ship.

**7.5** A description of the engine's on-board verification procedure shall be included in the approved method file.

**7.6** After installation of the approved method, a survey shall be conducted in accordance with the approved method file. If this survey confirms compliance, the Administration shall amend the ship's IAPP Certificate accordingly.

# *Appendix I*

## Form of EIAPP Certificate

*(Refer to 2.2.10 of the $NO_x$ Technical Code 2008)*

**ENGINE INTERNATIONAL AIR POLLUTION PREVENTION CERTIFICATE**

Issued under the provisions of the Protocol of 1997, as amended by resolution MEPC.176(58) in 2008, to amend the International Convention for the Prevention of Pollution from Ships, 1973, as modified by the Protocol of 1978 related thereto (hereinafter referred to as "the Convention") under the authority of the Government of:

. . . . . . . . . . . . . . . . . . . . . . . . . . . . . . . . . . . . . . . . . . . . .

*(Full designation of the country)*

by . . . . . . . . . . . . . . . . . . . . . . . . . . . . . . . . . . . . . . . . . . . .

*(Full designation of the competent person or organization authorized under the provisions of the Convention)*

| Engine manufacturer | Model number | Serial number | Test cycle(s) | Rated power (kW) and speed (rpm) | Engine approval number |
|---|---|---|---|---|---|
| | | | | | |

THIS IS TO CERTIFY:

1. That the above-mentioned marine diesel engine has been surveyed for pre-certification in accordance with the requirements of the Technical Code on Control of Emission of Nitrogen Oxides from Marine Diesel Engines 2008 made mandatory by Annex VI of the Convention; and

2. That the pre-certification survey shows that the engine, its components, adjustable features, and technical file, prior to the engine's installation and/or service on board a ship, fully comply with the applicable regulation 13 of Annex VI of the Convention.

This certificate is valid for the life of the engine subject to surveys in accordance with regulation 5 of Annex VI of the Convention, installed in ships under the authority of this Government.

Issued at: . . . . . . . . . . . . . . . . . . . . . . . . . . . . . . . . . . . . . . . . . .
*(Place of issue of certificate)*

(dd/mm/yyyy): . . . . . . . . . . . . . . . . . . . . . . . . . . . . . . . . . . . . . . .
*(Date of issue)* *(Signature of duly authorized official issuing the certificate)*

*(Seal or stamp of the authority, as appropriate)*

## SUPPLEMENT TO ENGINE INTERNATIONAL AIR POLLUTION PREVENTION CERTIFICATE (EIAPP CERTIFICATE)

### RECORD OF CONSTRUCTION, TECHNICAL FILE AND MEANS OF VERIFICATION

*Notes:*

1 This Record and its attachments shall be permanently attached to the EIAPP Certificate. The EIAPP Certificate shall accompany the engine throughout its life and shall be available on board the ship at all times.

2 The Record shall be at least in English, French or Spanish. If an official language of the issuing country is also used, this shall prevail in case of a dispute or discrepancy.

3 Unless otherwise stated, regulations mentioned in this Record refer to regulations of Annex VI of the Convention and the requirements for an engine's technical file and means of verifications refer to mandatory requirements from the revised $NO_x$ Technical Code 2008.

**1 Particulars of the engine**

1.1 Name and address of manufacturer. . . . . . . . . . . . . . . . . . .

1.2 Place of engine build . . . . . . . . . . . . . . . . . . . . . . . . . . . .

1.3 Date of engine build . . . . . . . . . . . . . . . . . . . . . . . . . . . . .

1.4 Place of pre-certification survey . . . . . . . . . . . . . . . . . . . .

1.5 Date of pre-certification survey. . . . . . . . . . . . . . . . . . . . . . . . . .

1.6 Engine type and model number . . . . . . . . . . . . . . . . . . . . . . . .

1.7 Engine serial number . . . . . . . . . . . . . . . . . . . . . . . . . . . . . .

1.8 If applicable, the engine is a parent engine □ or a member engine □ of the following engine family □ or engine group □. . . . . . . . . . . . . . . . . . . . . . . . . . . . . . . . . . . . . . . . . . . . . .

1.9 Individual engine or engine family / engine group details:

1.9.1 Approval reference . . . . . . . . . . . . . . . . . . . . . . . . . . . . . .

1.9.2 Rated power (kW) and rated speed (rpm) values or ranges . . . . . . . . . . . . . . . . . . . . . . . . . . . . . . . . . . . . . . . . . . . .

1.9.3 Test cycle(s) . . . . . . . . . . . . . . . . . . . . . . . . . . . . . . . . . .

1.9.4 Parent engine(s) test fuel oil specification . . . . . . . . . . . . . .

1.9.5 Applicable $NO_x$ emission limit (g/kWh), regulation 13.3, 13.4, or 13.5.1 (delete as appropriate) . . . . . . . . . . . . . . . . . . . . . .

1.9.6 Parent engine(s) emission value (g/kWh) . . . . . . . . . . . . .

## 2 Particulars of the technical file

The technical file, as required by chapter 2 of the $NO_x$ Technical Code 2008, is an essential part of the EIAPP Certificate and must always accompany an engine throughout its life and always be available on board a ship.

2.1 Technical file identification/approval number . . . . . . . . . . . .

2.2 Technical file approval date . . . . . . . . . . . . . . . . . . . . . . . . .

## 3 Specifications for the onboard $NO_x$ verification procedures

The specifications for the onboard $NO_x$ verification procedures, as required by chapter 6 of the $NO_x$ Technical Code 2008, are an essential part of the EIAPP Certificate and must always accompany an engine through its life and always be available on board a ship.

3.1 Engine parameter check method:

3.1.1 Identification/approval number. . . . . . . . . . . . . . . . . . . . . .

3.1.2 Approval date . . . . . . . . . . . . . . . . . . . . . . . . . . . . . . . . .

3.2 Direct measurement and monitoring method:

3.2.1 Identification/approval number. . . . . . . . . . . . . . . . . . . . .

3.2.2 Approval date . . . . . . . . . . . . . . . . . . . . . . . . . . . . . . . . . .

Alternatively the simplified measurement method in accordance with 6.3 of the $NO_x$ Technical Code 2008 may be utilized.

Issued at: . . . . . . . . . . . . . . . . . . . . . . . . . . . . . . . . . . . . . . . . .
*(Place of issue of certificate)*

(dd/mm/yyyy): . . . . . . . . . . . . . . . *(Date of issue)*

. . . . . . . . . . . . . . . . . . . . . . . . *(Signature of duly authorized official issuing the certificate)*

*(Seal or stamp of the authority, as appropriate)*

# *Appendix II*

## Flowcharts for survey and certification of marine diesel engines

*(Refer to 2.2.9 and 2.3.11 of the $NO_x$ Technical Code 2008)*

Guidance for compliance with survey and certification of marine diesel engines, as described in chapter 2 of this Code, is given in figures 1, 2 and 3 of this appendix:

Figure 1: Pre-certification survey at the manufacturer's facility

Figure 2: Initial survey on board a ship

Figure 3: Renewal, annual or intermediate survey on board a ship

*Note:* These flowcharts do not show the criteria for the certification of an existing engine as required by regulation 13.7.

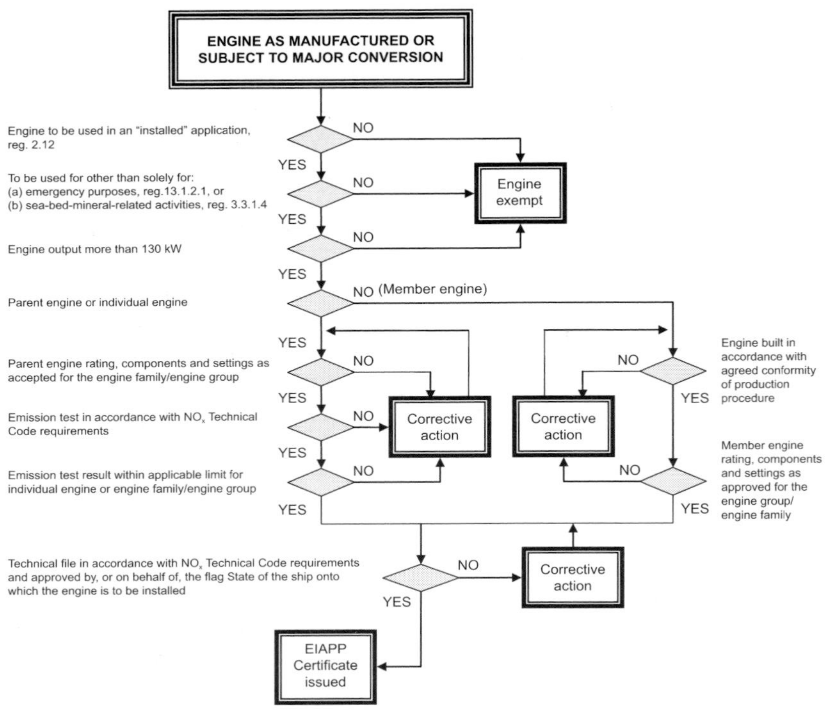


*Figure 1* – Pre-certification survey at the manufacturer's facility

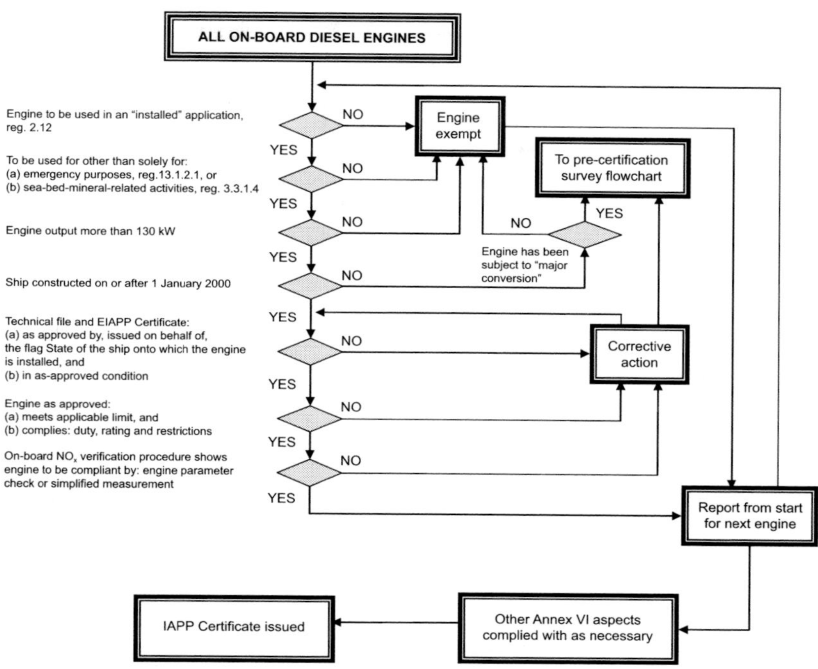


*Figure 2* – Initial survey on board a ship

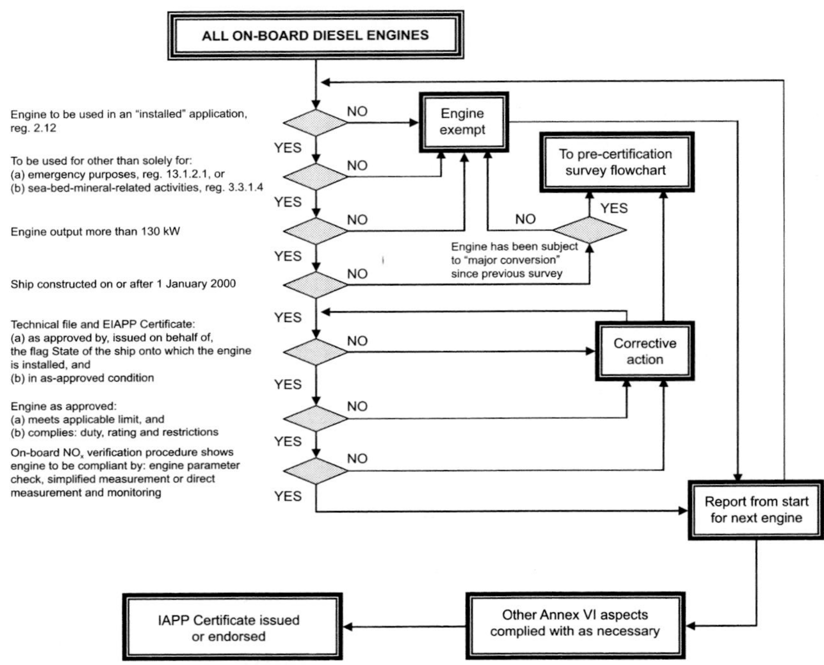


*Figure 3* – Renewal, annual or intermediate survey on board a ship

# *Appendix III*

## Specifications for analysers to be used in the determination of gaseous components of marine diesel engine emissions

*(Refer to chapter 5 of the $NO_x$ Technical Code 2008)*

### 1 General

**1.1** The components included in an exhaust gas analysis system for the determination of the concentrations of CO, $CO_2$, $NO_x$, HC and $O_2$ are shown in figure 1. All components in the sampling gas path must be maintained at the temperatures specified for the respective systems.

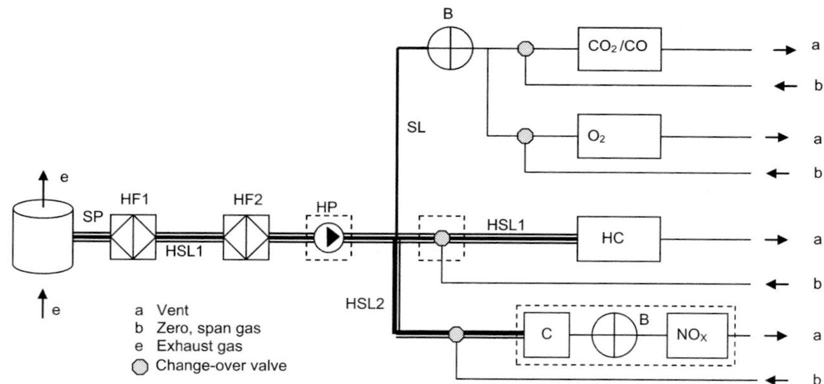


*Figure 1* – Arrangement of exhaust gas analysis system

**1.2** An exhaust gas analysis system shall include the following components. In accordance with chapter 5 of this Code equivalent arrangements and components may, subject to approval by the Administration, be accepted.

**.1** SP – Raw exhaust gas sampling probe

A stainless steel, straight, closed-end, multi-hole probe. The inside diameter shall not be greater than the inside diameter of the sampling line. The wall thickness of the probe should not be greater than 1 mm. There should be a minimum of three holes in three different radial planes sized to sample approximately the same flow.

For the raw exhaust gas, the sample for all components may be taken with one sampling probe or with two sampling probes located in close proximity and internally split to the different analysers.

*Note:* If exhaust pulsations or engine vibrations are likely to affect the sampling probe, the wall thickness of the probe may be enlarged subject to the approval of the Administration.

**.2** HSL1 – Heated sampling line

The sampling line provides a gas sample from a single probe to the split point(s) and the HC analyser. The sampling line shall be made of stainless steel or polytetrafluoroethylene (PTFE) and have a 4 mm minimum and a 13.5 mm maximum inside diameter.

The exhaust gas temperature at the sampling probe shall not be less than 190°C. The temperature of the exhaust gas from the sampling point to the analyser shall be maintained by using a heated filter and a heated transfer line with a wall temperature of 190°C ± 10°C.

If the temperature of the exhaust gas at the sampling probe is above 190°C, a wall temperature greater than 180°C shall be maintained.

Immediately before the heated filter and the HC analyser a gas temperature of 190°C ± 10°C shall be maintained.

**.3** HSL2 – Heated $NO_x$ sampling line

The sampling line shall be made of stainless steel or PTFE and maintain a wall temperature of 55°C to 200°C, up to the converter C when using a cooling unit B, and up to the analyser when a cooling unit B is not used.

**.4** HF1 – Heated pre-filter (optional)

The required temperature shall be the same as for HSL1.

**.5** HF2 – Heated filter

The filter shall extract any solid particles from the gas sample before the analyser. The temperature shall be the same as for HSL1. The filter shall be changed as necessary.

**.6** HP – Heated sampling pump (optional)

The pump shall be heated to the temperature of HSL1.

**.7** SL – Sampling line for CO, $CO_2$ and $O_2$

The line shall be made of PTFE or stainless steel. It may be heated or unheated.

**.8** $CO_2$/CO – Carbon dioxide and carbon monoxide analysers

Non-dispersive infrared (NDIR) absorption. Either separate analysers or two functions incorporated into a single analyser unit.

**.9** HC – Hydrocarbon analyser

Heated flame ionization detector (HFID). The temperature shall be kept at 180°C to 200°C.

**.10** $NO_x$ – Nitrogen oxides analyser

Chemiluminescent detector (CLD) or heated chemiluminescent detector (HCLD). If an HCLD is used, it shall be kept at a temperature of 55°C to 200°C.

*Note:* In the arrangement shown $NO_x$ is measured on a dry basis. $NO_x$ may also be measured on a wet basis, in which case the analyser shall be of the HCLD type.

**.11** C – Converter

A converter shall be used for the catalytic reduction of $NO_2$ to NO prior to analysis in the CLD or HCLD.

**.12** $O_2$ – Oxygen analyser

Paramagnetic detector (PMD), zirconium dioxide (ZRDO) or electrochemical sensor (ECS).

*Note:* In the arrangement shown $O_2$ is measured on a dry basis. $O_2$ may also be measured on a wet basis, in which case the analyser shall be of the ZRDO type.

**.13** B – Cooling unit

To cool and condense water from the exhaust sample. The cooler shall be maintained at a temperature of 0°C to 4°C by ice or refrigerator. If water is removed by condensation, the sample gas temperature or dew point shall be monitored either within the water trap or downstream. The sample gas temperature or dew point shall not exceed 7°C.

**1.3** The analysers shall have a measuring range appropriate for the accuracy required to measure the concentrations of the exhaust gas components (see 1.6) and 5.9.7.1 of this Code. It is recommended that the analysers be operated such that the measured concentration falls between 15% and 100% of full scale, where full scale refers to the measurement range used.

**1.4** If the full-scale value is 155 ppm (or ppmC) or less, or if read-out systems (computers, data loggers) that provide sufficient accuracy and resolution below 15% of full scale are used, concentrations below 15% of full scale are also acceptable. In this case, additional calibrations are to be made to ensure the accuracy of the calibration curves.

**1.5** The electromagnetic compatibility (EMC) of the equipment shall be such as to minimize additional errors.

**1.6** *Accuracy*

**1.6.1** Definitions

ISO 5725-1:1994/Cor 1:1998, Accuracy (trueness and precision) of measurement methods and results – Part 1: General principles and definitions, Technical Corrigendum 1.

ISO 5725-2:1994, Accuracy (trueness and precision) of measurement methods and results – Part 2: Basic method for the determination of repeatability and reproducibility of a standard measurement method.

**1.6.2** An analyser shall not deviate from the nominal calibration point by more than ± 2% of the reading over the whole measurement range except zero, or ± 0.3% of full scale, whichever is larger. The accuracy shall be determined according to the calibration requirements laid down in section 5 of appendix IV of this Code.

**1.7** *Precision*

The precision, defined as 2.5 times the standard deviation of 10 repetitive responses to a given calibration or span gas, shall be not greater than ± 1% of full-scale concentration for each range used above 100 ppm (or ppmC) or ± 2% of each range used below 100 ppm (or ppmC).

### 1.8 *Noise*

The analyser peak-to-peak response to zero and calibration or span gases over any 10-second period shall not exceed 2% of full scale on all ranges used.

### 1.9 *Zero drift*

Zero response is defined as the mean response, including noise, to a zero gas during a 30-second time interval. The drift of the zero response during a one-hour period shall be less than 2% of full scale on the lowest range used.

### 1.10 *Span drift*

Span response is defined as the mean response, including noise, to a span gas during a 30-second time interval. The drift of the span response during a one-hour period shall be less than 2% of full scale on the lowest range used.

## 2 Gas drying

Exhaust gases may be measured wet or dry. A gas-drying device, if used, shall have a minimal effect on the composition of the measured gases. Chemical dryers are not an acceptable method of removing water from the sample.

## 3 Analysers

Sections 3.1 to 3.5 describe the measurement principles to be used. The gases to be measured shall be analysed with the following instruments. For non-linear analysers, the use of linearizing circuits is permitted.

### 3.1 *Carbon monoxide (CO) analysis*

The carbon monoxide analyser shall be of the non-dispersive infrared (NDIR) absorption type.

### 3.2 *Carbon dioxide ($CO_2$) analysis*

The carbon dioxide analyser shall be of the non-dispersive infrared (NDIR) absorption type.

### 3.3 *Hydrocarbon (HC) analysis*

The hydrocarbon analyser shall be of the heated flame ionization detector (HFID) type with detector, valves, pipework and associated components heated so as to maintain a gas temperature of 190°C ± 10°C.

### 3.4 *Nitrogen oxides ($NO_x$) analysis*

The nitrogen oxides analyser shall be of the chemiluminescent detector (CLD) or heated chemiluminescent detector (HCLD) type with an $NO_2$/NO converter, if measured on a dry basis. If measured on a wet basis, an HCLD with converter maintained above 55°C shall be used, provided the water quench check (see section 9.2.2 of appendix IV of this Code) is satisfied. For both CLD and HCLD, the sampling path shall be maintained at a wall temperature of 55°C to 200°C up to the converter for dry measurement, and up to the analyser for wet measurement.

### 3.5 *Oxygen ($O_2$) analysis*

The oxygen analyser shall be of the paramagnetic detector (PMD), zirconium dioxide (ZRDO) or electrochemical sensor (ECS) type.

# *Appendix IV*

## Calibration of the analytical and measurement instruments

*(Refer to chapters 5 and 6 of the $NO_x$ Technical Code 2008)*

### 1 Introduction

**1.1** Each analyser used for the measurement of an engine's parameters shall be calibrated as often as necessary in accordance with the requirements of this appendix.

**1.2** Except as otherwise specified, all results of measurements, test data or calculations required by this appendix shall be recorded in the engine's test report in accordance with section 5.10 of this Code.

**1.3** *Accuracy of measuring instruments*

**1.3.1** The calibration of all measuring instruments shall comply with the requirements as set out in tables 1, 2, 3 and 4 and shall be traceable to standards recognized by the Administration. Additional engine measurements may be required by the Administration, and such additional measuring instruments used shall comply with the appropriate deviation standard and calibration validity period.

**1.3.2** The instruments shall be calibrated:

**.1** in time intervals not greater than as given in tables 1, 2, 3 and 4; or

**.2** in accordance with alternative calibration procedures and validity periods subject to such proposals being submitted in advance of the tests and approved by the Administration.

*Note:* The deviations given in tables 1, 2, 3, and 4 refer to the final recorded value, which is inclusive of the data acquisition system.

*Table 1* – Permissible deviations and calibration validity periods of instruments for engine-related parameters for measurements on a test bed

| No. | Measurement instrument | Permissible deviation | Calibration validity period (months) |
|---|---|---|---|
| 1 | Engine speed | ± 2% of reading or ± 1% of engine's maximum value, whichever is larger | 3 |
| 2 | Torque | ± 2% of reading or ± 1% of engine's maximum value, whichever is larger | 3 |
| 3 | Power (where measured directly) | ± 2% of reading or ± 1% of engine's maximum value, whichever is larger | 3 |
| 4 | Fuel consumption | ± 2% of engine's maximum value | 6 |
| 5 | Air consumption | ± 2% of reading or ± 1% of engine's maximum value, whichever is larger | 6 |
| 6 | Exhaust gas flow | ± 2.5% of reading or ± 1.5% of engine's maximum value, whichever is larger | 6 |

*Table 2* – Permissible deviations and calibration interval periods of instruments for other essential parameters for measurements on a test bed

| No. | Measurement instrument | Permissible deviation | Calibration validity period (months) |
|---|---|---|---|
| 1 | Temperatures $\leq 327°C$ | ± 2°C absolute | 3 |
| 2 | Temperatures $> 327°C$ | ± 1% of reading | 3 |

| No. | Measurement instrument | Permissible deviation | Calibration validity period (months) |
|---|---|---|---|
| 3 | Exhaust gas pressure | ± 0.2 kPa absolute | 3 |
| 4 | Charge air pressure | ± 0.3 kPa absolute | 3 |
| 5 | Atmospheric pressure | ± 0.1 kPa absolute | 3 |
| 6 | Other pressures ≤ 1000 kPa | ± 20 kPa absolute | 3 |
| 7 | Other pressures > 1000 kPa | ± 2% of reading | 3 |
| 8 | Relative humidity | ± 3% absolute | 1 |

*Table 3* – Permissible deviations and calibration validity periods of instruments for engine-related parameters for measurements on board a ship when the engine is already pre-certified

| No. | Measurement instrument | Permissible deviation | Calibration validity period (months) |
|---|---|---|---|
| 1 | Engine speed | ± 2% of engine's maximum value | 12 |
| 2 | Torque | ± 5% of engine's maximum value | 12 |
| 3 | Power (where measured directly) | ± 5% of engine's maximum value | 12 |
| 4 | Fuel consumption | ± 4% of engine's maximum value | 12 |
| 5 | Air consumption | ± 5% of engine's maximum value | 12 |
| 6 | Exhaust gas flow | ± 5% of engine's maximum value | 12 |

*Table 4* – Permissible deviations and calibration validity periods of instruments for other essential parameters for measurements on board a ship when the engine is already pre-certified

| No. | Measurement instrument | Permissible deviation | Calibration validity period (months) |
|---|---|---|---|
| 1 | Temperatures $\leq 327°C$ | $\pm$ 2°C absolute | 12 |
| 2 | Temperatures $> 327°C$ | $\pm$ 15°C absolute | 12 |
| 3 | Exhaust gas pressure | $\pm$ 5% of engine's maximum value | 12 |
| 4 | Charge air pressure | $\pm$ 5% of engine's maximum value | 12 |
| 5 | Atmospheric pressure | $\pm$ 0.5% of reading | 12 |
| 6 | Other pressures | $\pm$ 5 % of reading | 12 |
| 7 | Relative humidity | $\pm$ 3% absolute | 6 |

## 2 Calibration gases and zero and span check gases

The shelf life of all calibration gases and span and zero check gases shall be respected. The expiry date of the calibration gases and the zero and span check gases, stated by the manufacturer, shall be recorded.

### 2.1 *Pure gases (including zero check gases)*

**2.1.1** The required purity of the gases is defined by the contamination limits given below. The following gases shall be available:

- **.1** purified nitrogen (contamination $\leq$ 1 ppmC, $\leq$ 1 ppm CO, $\leq$ 400 ppm $CO_2$, $\leq$ 0.1 ppm NO);
- **.2** purified oxygen (purity $>$ 99.5% volume $O_2$);
- **.3** hydrogen-helium mixture (40 $\pm$ 2% $H_2$, balance He), (contamination $\leq$ 1 ppmC, $\leq$ 400 ppm $CO_2$); and

**.4** purified synthetic air (contamination $\leq$ 1 ppmC, $\leq$ 1 ppm CO, $\leq$ 400 ppm $CO_2$, $\leq$ 0.1 ppm NO (oxygen content 18% – 21% volume).

**2.2** *Calibration and span gases*

**2.2.1** Mixtures of gases having the following chemical compositions shall be available:

**.1** CO and purified nitrogen;

**.2** $NO_x$ and purified nitrogen (the amount of $NO_2$ contained in this calibration gas shall not exceed 5% of the NO content);

**.3** $O_2$ and purified nitrogen;

**.4** $CO_2$ and purified nitrogen; and

**.5** $CH_4$ and purified synthetic air, or $C_3H_8$ and purified synthetic air.

*Note:* Other gas combinations are allowed, provided the gases do not react with one another.

**2.2.2** The true concentration of a calibration and span gas must be within ± 2% of the nominal value. All concentrations of calibration and span gases shall be given on a volume basis (volume per cent or volume ppm).

**2.2.3** The gases used for calibration and span may also be obtained by means of precision blending devices (gas dividers), diluting with purified $N_2$ or with purified synthetic air. The accuracy of the mixing device must be such that the concentration of the blended calibration gases is accurate to within ± 2%. This accuracy implies that primary gases used for blending must be known to an accuracy of at least ± 1%, traceable to national or international gas standards. The verification shall be performed at between 15 and 50% of full scale for each calibration incorporating a blending device. Optionally, the blending device may be checked with an instrument that by nature is linear, e.g., using NO gas with a CLD. The span value of the instrument shall be adjusted with the span gas directly connected to the instrument. The blending device shall be checked at the used settings, and the nominal value shall be compared to the measured concentration of the instrument. This difference shall in each point be within ± 1% of the nominal value. This linearity check of the gas divider shall not be performed with a gas analyser that was previously linearized with the same gas divider.

**2.2.4** Oxygen interference check gases shall contain propane or methane with 350 ppmC ± 75 ppmC hydrocarbons. The concentration shall be determined to calibration gas tolerances by chromatographic analysis of total hydrocarbons plus impurities or by dynamic bleeding. Nitrogen shall be the predominant diluent with the balance oxygen. Blends required are listed in table 5.

*Table 5* – Oxygen interference check gases

| $O_2$ concentration | Balance |
|---|---|
| 21 (20 to 22) | Nitrogen |
| 10 (9 to 11) | Nitrogen |
| 5 (4 to 6) | Nitrogen |

## 3 Operating procedure for analysers and sampling system

The operating procedure for analysers shall follow the start-up and operating instructions of the instrument manufacturer. The minimum requirements given in sections 4 to 9 shall be included.

## 4 Leakage test

**4.1** A system leakage test shall be performed. The probe shall be disconnected from the exhaust system and the end plugged. The analyser pump shall be switched on. After an initial stabilization period all flow meters shall read zero. If not, the sampling lines shall be checked and the fault corrected.

**4.2** The maximum allowable leakage rate on the vacuum side shall be 0.5% of the in-use flow rate for the portion of the system being checked. The analyser flows and bypass flows may be used to estimate the in-use flow rates.

**4.3** Another method is the introduction of a concentration step change at the beginning of the sampling line by switching from zero to span gas. If, after an adequate period of time, the reading shows a lower concentration compared to the introduced concentration, this points to calibration or leakage problems.

**4.4** Other arrangements may be acceptable subject to approval of the Administration.

## 5 Calibration procedure

**5.1** *Instrument assembly*

The instrument assembly shall be calibrated and the calibration curves checked against standard gases. The same gas flow rates shall be used as when sampling exhaust.

**5.2** *Warming-up time*

The warming-up time shall be according to the recommendations of the analyser's manufacturer. If not specified, a minimum of two hours is recommended for warming up the analysers.

**5.3** *NDIR and HFID analysers*

The NDIR analyser shall be tuned as necessary. The HFID flame shall be optimized as necessary.

**5.4** *Calibration*

**5.4.1** Each normally used operating range shall be calibrated. Analysers shall be calibrated not more than 3 months before being used for testing or whenever a system repair or change is made that can influence calibration, or as per provided for by 1.3.2.2.

**5.4.2** Using purified synthetic air (or nitrogen) the CO, $CO_2$, $NO_x$ and $O_2$ analysers shall be set at zero. The HFID analyser shall be set to zero using purified synthetic air.

**5.4.3** The appropriate calibration gases shall be introduced to the analysers, the values recorded, and the calibration curve established accordingly.

**5.5** *Establishment of the calibration curve*

**5.5.1** General guidance

**5.5.1.1** The calibration curve shall be established by at least 6 calibration points (excluding zero) approximately equally spaced over the operating range from zero to the highest value expected during emissions testing.

**5.5.1.2** The calibration curve shall be calculated by the method of least squares. A best-fit linear or non-linear equation may be used.

**5.5.1.3** The calibration points shall not differ from the least-squares best-fit line by more than ± 2% of reading or ± 0.3% of full scale, whichever is larger.

**5.5.1.4** The zero setting shall be rechecked and the calibration procedure repeated, if necessary.

**5.5.1.5** If it can be shown that alternative calibration methods (e.g., computer, electronically controlled range switch, etc.) can give equivalent accuracy, then these alternatives may be used subject to the approval by the Administration.

## 6 Verification of the calibration

**6.1** Each normally used operating range shall be checked prior to each analysis in accordance with the following procedure:

- **.1** the calibration shall be checked by using a zero gas and a span gas whose nominal value shall be more than 80% of full scale of the measuring range; and
- **.2** if, for the two points considered, the value found does not differ by more than ± 4% of full scale from the declared reference value, the adjustment parameters may be modified. If this is not the case, a new calibration curve shall be established in accordance with 5.5 above.

## 7 Efficiency test of the $NO_x$ converter

The efficiency of the converter used for the conversion of $NO_2$ into NO shall be tested as given in 7.1 to 7.10 below.

### 7.1 *Test set-up*

Using the test set-up as schematically shown in figure 1 and the procedure below, the efficiency of converter shall be tested by means of an ozonator.

### 7.2 *Calibration*

The CLD and the HCLD shall be calibrated in the most common operating range following the manufacturer's specifications using zero and span gas (the NO content of which must amount to about 80% of the operating range and the $NO_2$ concentration of the gas mixture to less than 5% of the NO concentration). The $NO_x$ analyser must be in the NO mode so that the span gas does not pass through the converter. The indicated concentration shall be recorded.

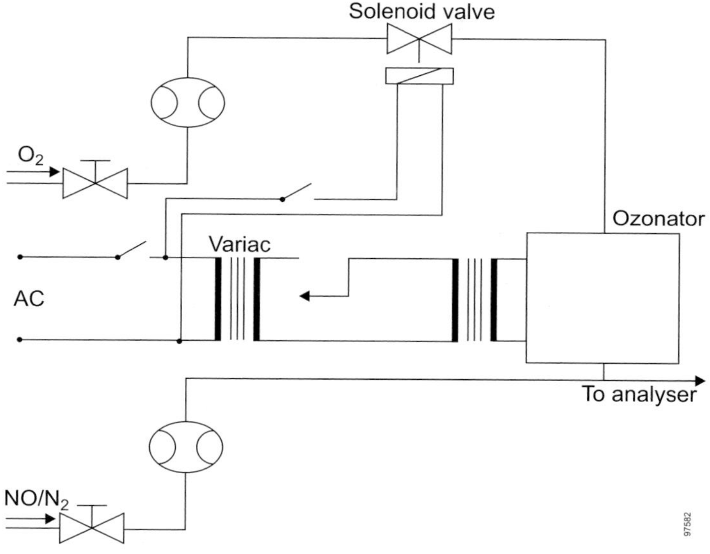


*Figure 1* – Schematic representation of $NO_2$ converter efficiency device

### 7.3 *Calculation*

The efficiency of the $NO_x$ converter shall be calculated as follows:

$$E_{NO_x} = \left(1 + \frac{a-b}{c-d}\right) \cdot 100 \qquad (1)$$

where:

$a$ = $NO_x$ concentration according to 7.6 below

$b$ = $NO_x$ concentration according to 7.7 below

$c$ = NO concentration according to 7.4 below

$d$ = NO concentration according to 7.5 below

### **7.4** *Adding of oxygen*

**7.4.1** Via a T-fitting, oxygen or zero air is added continuously to the gas flow until the concentration indicated is about 20% less than the indicated calibration concentration given in 7.2 above. The analyser must be in the NO mode.

**7.4.2** The indicated concentration (*c*) shall be recorded. The ozonator must be kept deactivated throughout the process.

### **7.5** *Activation of the ozonator*

The ozonator shall then be activated to generate enough ozone to bring the NO concentration down to about 20% (minimum 10%) of the calibration concentration given in 7.2 above. The indicated concentration (*d*) shall be recorded. The analyser must be in the NO mode.

### **7.6** *$NO_x$ mode*

The NO analyser shall then be switched to the $NO_x$ mode so that the gas mixture (consisting of NO, $NO_2$, $O_2$ and $N_2$) now passes through the converter. The indicated concentration (*a*) shall be recorded. The analyser must be in the $NO_x$ mode.

### **7.7** *Deactivation of the ozonator*

The ozonator is then deactivated. The mixture of gases described in 7.6 above passes through the converter into the detector. The indicated concentration (*b*) shall be recorded. The analyser is in the $NO_x$ mode.

### **7.8** *NO mode*

Switched to NO mode with the ozonator deactivated, the flow of oxygen or synthetic air shall also be shut off. The $NO_x$ reading of the analyser shall not deviate by more than 5% from the value measured according to 7.2 above. The analyser must be in the NO mode.

### **7.9** *Test interval*

The efficiency of the converter shall be tested prior to each calibration of the $NO_x$ analyser.

**7.10** *Efficiency requirement*

The efficiency of the converter shall not be less than 90%.

## 8 Adjustment of the HFID

**8.1** *Optimization of the detector response*

**8.1.1** The HFID shall be adjusted as specified by the instrument manufacturer. A propane-in-air span gas shall be used to optimize the response on the most common operating range.

**8.1.2** With the fuel and air flow rates set at the manufacturer's recommendations, a 350 ± 75 ppmC span gas shall be introduced to the analyser. The response at a given fuel flow shall be determined from the difference between the span gas response and the zero gas response. The fuel flow shall be incrementally adjusted above and below the manufacturer's specification. The span and zero response at these fuel flows shall be recorded. The difference between the span and zero response shall be plotted and the fuel flow adjusted to the rich side of the curve. This is the initial flow rate setting, which may need further optimization depending on the results of the hydrocarbon response factors and the oxygen interference check according to 8.2 and 8.3.

**8.1.3** If the oxygen interference or the hydrocarbon response factors do not meet the following specifications, the air flow shall be incrementally adjusted above and below the manufacturer's specifications, 8.2 and 8.3 for each flow.

**8.1.4** The optimization may optionally be conducted using alternative procedures subject to the approval of the Administration.

**8.2** *Hydrocarbon response factors*

**8.2.1** The analyser shall be calibrated using propane in air and purified synthetic air, according to 5.

**8.2.2** Response factors shall be determined when introducing an analyser into service and after major service intervals. The response factor ($r_h$) for a particular hydrocarbon species is the ratio of the HFID ppmC reading to the gas concentration in the cylinder expressed in terms of ppmC.

**8.2.3** The concentration of the test gas must be at a level to give a response of approximately 80% of full scale. The concentration must be known to an accuracy of ± 2% in reference to a gravimetric standard expressed in volume. In addition, the gas cylinder must be preconditioned for 24 hours at a temperature of 25°C ± 5°C.

**8.2.4** The test gases to be used and the recommended relative response factor ranges are as follows:

- Methane and purified synthetic air $1.00 \leq r_h \leq 1.15$
- Propylene and purified synthetic air $0.90 \leq r_h \leq 1.1$
- Toluene and purified synthetic air $0.90 \leq r_h \leq 1.1$

These values are relative to an $r_h$ of 1 for propane and purified synthetic air.

**8.3** *Oxygen interference check*

**8.3.1** The oxygen interference check shall be determined when introducing an analyser into service and after major service intervals.

**8.3.2** A range shall be chosen where the oxygen interference check gases will fall in the upper 50%. The test shall be conducted with the oven temperature set as required. The oxygen interference gases are specified in 2.2.4.

**.1** The analyser shall be zeroed.

**.2** The analyser shall be spanned with the 21% oxygen blend.

**.3** The zero response shall be re-checked. If it has changed more than 0.5% of full scale (FS), steps 8.3.2.1 and 8.3.2.2 shall be repeated.

**.4** The 5% and 10% oxygen interference check gases shall be introduced.

**.5** The zero response shall be rechecked. If it has changed more than ± 1% of full scale, the test shall be repeated.

**.6** The oxygen interference ($\%O_2I$) shall be calculated for each mixture in step .4 as follows:

$$\%O_2I = \frac{(B - \text{analyser response})}{B} \cdot 100 \qquad (2)$$

where:

analyser response is $(A/\%\text{FS at } A) \cdot (\%\text{FS at } B)$

where:

$A$ = hydrocarbon concentration in ppmC (microlitres per litre) of the span gas used in 8.3.2.2

$B$ = hydrocarbon concentration (ppmC) of the oxygen interference check gases used in 8.3.2.4

$$(\text{ppmC}) = \frac{A}{D} \tag{3}$$

where:

D = percentage of full-scale analyser response due to A

**.7** The % of oxygen interference ($\%O_2I$) shall be less than ± 3.0% for all required oxygen interference check gases prior to testing.

**.8** If the oxygen interference is greater than ± 3.0%, the air flow above and below the manufacturer's specifications shall be incrementally adjusted, repeating 8.1 for each flow.

**.9** If the oxygen interference is greater than ± 3.0% after adjusting the air flow, the fuel flow, and thereafter the sample flow, shall be varied, repeating 8.1 for each new setting.

**.10** If the oxygen interference is still greater than ± 3.0%, the analyser, HFID fuel, or burner air shall be repaired or replaced prior to testing. This clause shall then be repeated with the repaired or replaced equipment or gases.

## 9 Interference effects with CO, $CO_2$, $NO_x$ and $O_2$ analysers

Gases other than the one being analysed can interfere with the reading in several ways. Positive interference occurs in NDIR and PMD instruments where the interfering gas gives the same effect as the gas being measured, but to a lesser degree. Negative interference occurs in NDIR instruments by the interfering gas broadening the absorption band of the measured gas, and in CLD instruments by the interfering gas quenching the radiation. The interference checks in 9.1 and 9.2 shall be performed prior to an analyser's initial use and after major service intervals, but at least once per year.

### **9.1** *CO analyser interference check*

Water and $CO_2$ can interfere with the CO analyser performance. Therefore, a $CO_2$ span gas having a concentration of 80% to 100% of full scale of the maximum operating range used during testing shall be bubbled through water at room temperature and the analyser response recorded. The analyser response must not be more than 1% of full scale for ranges equal to or above 300 ppm or more than 3 ppm for ranges below 300 ppm.

### **9.2** *$NO_x$ analyser quench checks*

The two gases of concern for CLD (and HCLD) analysers are $CO_2$ and water vapour. Quench responses to these gases are proportional to their concentrations, and therefore require test techniques to determine the quench at the highest expected concentrations experienced during testing.

#### **9.2.1** $CO_2$ quench check

**9.2.1.1** A $CO_2$ span gas having a concentration of 80% to 100% of full scale of the maximum operating range shall be passed through the NDIR analyser and the $CO_2$ value recorded as $A$. It shall then be diluted approximately 50% with NO span gas and passed through the NDIR and (H)CLD, with the $CO_2$ and NO values recorded as $B$ and $C$, respectively. The $CO_2$ shall then be shut off and only the NO span gas be passed through the (H)CLD and the NO value recorded as $D$.

**9.2.1.2** The quench shall be calculated as follows:

$$E_{CO2} = \left[1 - \left(\frac{(C \cdot A)}{(D \cdot A) - (D \cdot B)}\right)\right] \cdot 100 \qquad (4)$$

where:

$A$ = the undiluted $CO_2$ concentration measured with NDIR in percentage by volume;

$B$ = the diluted $CO_2$ concentration measured with NDIR in percentage by volume;

$C$ = the diluted NO concentration measured with (H)CLD in ppm; and

$D$ = the undiluted NO concentration measured with (H)CLD in ppm.

**9.2.1.3** Alternative methods of diluting and quantifying of $CO_2$ and NO span gas values, such as dynamic mixing/blending, can be used.

**9.2.2** Water quench check

**9.2.2.1** This check applies to wet gas concentration measurements only. Calculation of water quench must consider dilution of the NO span gas with water vapour and scaling of water vapour concentration of the mixture to that expected during testing.

**9.2.2.2** An NO span gas having a concentration of 80% to 100% of full scale of the normal operating range shall be passed through the HCLD and the NO value recorded as $D$. The NO span gas shall then be bubbled through water at a temperature of 25°C ± 5°C and passed through the HCLD and the NO value recorded as $C$. The water temperature shall be determined and recorded as $F$. The mixture's saturation vapour pressure that corresponds to the bubbler water temperature ($F$) shall be determined and recorded as $G$. The water vapour concentration ($H$ in %) of the mixture shall be calculated as follows:

$$H = 100 \cdot \left(\frac{G}{p_b}\right) \tag{5}$$

The expected diluted NO span gas (in water vapour) concentration ($D_e$) shall be calculated as follows:

$$D_e = D \cdot \left(1 - \frac{H}{100}\right) \tag{6}$$

For diesel engine exhaust, the maximum exhaust water concentration (in %) expected during testing shall be estimated, under the assumption of a fuel atom H/C ratio of 1.8/1, from the maximum $CO_2$ concentration $A$ in the exhaust gas as follows:

$$H_m = 0.9 \cdot A \tag{7}$$

and $H_m$ is recorded.

**9.2.2.3** The water quench shall be calculated as follows:

$$E_{H2O} = 100 \cdot \left(\frac{D_e - C}{D_e}\right) \cdot \left(\frac{H_m}{H}\right) \tag{8}$$

where:

$D_e$ = the expected diluted NO concentration in ppm;

$C$ = the diluted NO concentration in ppm;

$H_m$ = the maximum water vapour concentration in %; and

$H$ = the actual water vapour concentration in %.

*Note:* It is important that the NO span gas contain minimal $NO_2$ concentration for this check, as absorption of $NO_2$ in water has not been accounted for in the quench calculations.

**9.2.3** Maximum allowable quench

The maximum allowable quench shall be:

**.1** $CO_2$ quench according to 9.2.1: 2% of full scale.

**.2** Water quench according to 9.2.2: 3% of full scale.

**9.3** *$O_2$ analyser interference*

**9.3.1** Instrument response of a PMD analyser caused by gases other than oxygen is comparatively slight. The oxygen equivalents of the common exhaust gas constituents are shown in table 6.

*Table 6* – Oxygen equivalents

| Gas | $O_2$ equivalent % |
|---|---|
| Carbon dioxide ($CO_2$) | – 0.623 |
| Carbon monoxide (CO) | – 0.354 |
| Nitric oxide (NO) | + 44.4 |
| Nitrogen dioxide ($NO_2$) | + 28.7 |
| Water ($H_2O$) | – 0.381 |

**9.3.2** The observed oxygen concentration shall be corrected by the following formula:

$$E_{O2} = \frac{(\text{Equivalent } O_2 \cdot c_{\text{observed}})}{100} \qquad (9)$$

**9.3.3** For ZRDO and ECS analysers, instrument interference caused by gases other than oxygen shall be compensated in accordance with the manufacturer's recommendations and with good engineering practice. Electrochemical sensors shall be compensated for $CO_2$ and $NO_x$ interference.

# *Appendix V*

## Parent engine test report and test data

*(Refer to 2.4.1.5 and 5.10 of the $NO_x$ Technical Code 2008)*

## Section 1 – Parent engine test report – see 5.10 of the Code

**Emissions test report no. ................** **Engine information** Sheet 1/5

| **Engine** | | | | |
|---|---|---|---|---|
| Manufacturer | | | | |
| Engine type | | | | |
| Engine family or engine group identification | | | | |
| Serial number | | | | |
| Rated speed | | rpm | | |
| Rated power | | kW | | |
| Intermediate speed | | rpm | | |
| Maximum torque at intermediate speed | | Nm | | |
| Static injection timing | | deg CA BTDC | | |
| Electronic injection control | No: | Yes: | | |
| Variable injection timing | No: | Yes: | | |
| Variable turbocharger geometry | No: | Yes: | | |
| Bore | | mm | | |
| Stroke | | mm | | |
| Nominal compression ratio | | | | |
| Mean effective pressure, at rated power | | kPa | | |
| Maximum cylinder pressure, at rated power | | kPa | | |
| Cylinder number and configuration | Number: | V: | In-line: | |
| Auxiliaries | | | | |
| **Specified ambient conditions** | | | | |
| Maximum seawater temperature | | °C | | |
| Maximum charge air temperature, if applicable | | °C | | |
| Cooling system spec. intermediate cooler | No: | Yes: | | |
| Cooling system spec. charge air stages | | | | |
| Low/high temperature cooling system set points | / | °C | | |
| Maximum inlet depression | | kPa | | |
| Maximum exhaust backpressure | | kPa | | |
| Fuel oil specification | | | | |
| Fuel oil temperature | | °C | | |
| **Emissions test results** | | | | |
| Cycle | | | | |
| $NO_x$ | | | | g/kWh |
| Test identification | | | | |
| Date/time | | | | |
| Test site/bench | | | | |
| Test number | | | | |
| Surveyor | | | | |
| Date and place of report | | | | |
| Signature | | | | |

**Emissions test report no. ................** **Engine family information** Sheet 2/5

| **Engine family/engine group information (common specifications)** | |
|---|---|
| Combustion cycle | 2-stroke cycle/4-stroke cycle |
| Cooling medium | Air/Water |
| Cylinder configuration | Required to be written, only if the exhaust cleaning devices are applied |
| Method of aspiration | Natural aspired/Pressure charged |
| Fuel type to be used on board | Distillate/distillate or Heavy fuel/dual |
| Combustion chamber | Open chamber/Divided chamber |
| Valve port configuration | Cylinder head/Cylinder wall |
| Valve port size and number | |
| Fuel system type | |

| **Miscellaneous features** | |
|---|---|
| Exhaust gas re-circulation | No/Yes |
| Water injection/emulsion | No/Yes |
| Air injection | No/Yes |
| Charge cooling system | No/Yes |
| Exhaust after-treatment | No/Yes |
| Exhaust after-treatment type | |
| Dual fuel | No/Yes |

| **Engine family/engine group information (selection of parent engine for test-bed test)** | | | | | |
|---|---|---|---|---|---|
| Family/group identification | | | | | |
| Method of pressure charging | | | | | |
| Charge air cooling system | | | | | |
| Criteria of the selection of parent engine | Highest $NO_x$ emission value | | | | |
| Number of cylinders | | | | | |
| Maximum rated power per cylinder | | | | | |
| Rated speed | | | | | |
| Injection timing (range) | | | | | |
| Selected parent engine | | | | | Parent |
| Test cycle(s) | | | | | |

**Emissions test report no. ................** **Test cell information** Sheet 3/5

| **Exhaust pipe** | |
|---|---|
| Diameter | mm |
| Length | m |
| Insulation | No: Yes: |
| Probe location | |

| **Measurement equipment** | | | | | |
|---|---|---|---|---|---|
| | Manufacturer | Model | Measurement ranges | Calibration | |
| | | | | Span gas conc. | Deviation of calibration |
| **Analyser** | | | | | |
| $NO_x$ analyser | | | ppm | | % |
| CO analyser | | | ppm | | % |
| $CO_2$ analyser | | | % | | % |
| $O_2$ analyser | | | % | | % |
| HC analyser | | | ppmC | | % |
| Speed | | | rpm | | % |
| Torque | | | Nm | | % |
| Power, if applicable | | | kW | | % |
| Fuel flow | | | | | % |
| Air flow | | | | | % |
| Exhaust flow | | | | | % |
| **Temperatures** | | | | | |
| Charge air coolant inlet | | | °C | | °C |
| Exhaust gas | | | °C | | °C |
| Inlet air | | | °C | | °C |
| Charge air | | | °C | | °C |
| Fuel | | | °C | | °C |
| **Pressures** | | | | | |
| Exhaust gas | | | kPa | | kPa |
| Charge air | | | kPa | | kPa |
| Atmospheric | | | kPa | | kPa |
| **Vapour pressure** | | | | | |
| Intake air | | | kPa | | % |
| **Humidity** | | | | | |
| Intake air | | | % | | % |

**Fuel characteristics**

| **Fuel type** | | | | |
|---|---|---|---|---|
| **Fuel properties** | | | **Fuel elemental analysis** | |
| Density | ISO 3675 | $kg/m^3$ | Carbon | % m/m |
| Viscosity | ISO 3104 | $mm^2/s$ | Hydrogen | % m/m |
| Water | ISO 3733 | % V/V | Nitrogen | % m/m |
| | | | Oxygen | % m/m |
| | | | Sulphur | % m/m |
| | | | LHV/Hu | MJ/kg |

Emissions test report no. ................ **Ambient and gaseous emissions data** Sheet 4/5

| Mode | | 1 | 2 | 3 | 4 | 5 | 6 | 7 | 8 | 9 | 10 |
|---|---|---|---|---|---|---|---|---|---|---|---|
| Power/torque | % | | | | | | | | | | |
| Speed | % | | | | | | | | | | |
| Time at beginning of mode | | | | | | | | | | | |
| **Ambient data** | | | | | | | | | | | |
| Atmospheric pressure | kPa | | | | | | | | | | |
| Intake air temperature | °C | | | | | | | | | | |
| Intake air humidity | g/kg | | | | | | | | | | |
| Relative humidity (RH) of intake air* | % | | | | | | | | | | |
| Air temperature at RH sensor* | °C | | | | | | | | | | |
| Dry bulb temperature of intake air* | °C | | | | | | | | | | |
| Wet bulb temperature of intake air* | °C | | | | | | | | | | |
| Test condition parameter, $f_a$ | | | | | | | | | | | |
| **Gaseous emissions data** | | | | | | | | | | | |
| $NO_x$ concentration dry/wet | ppm | | | | | | | | | | |
| CO concentration | ppm | | | | | | | | | | |
| $CO_2$ concentration | % | | | | | | | | | | |
| $O_2$ concentration dry/wet | % | | | | | | | | | | |
| HC concentration | ppmC | | | | | | | | | | |
| $NO_x$ humidity correction factor, $k_{hd}$ | | | | | | | | | | | |
| Dry/wet correction factor, $k_{wr}$ | | | | | | | | | | | |
| $NO_x$ mass flow | kg/h | | | | | | | | | | |
| CO mass flow | kg/h | | | | | | | | | | |
| $CO_2$ mass flow | kg/h | | | | | | | | | | |
| $O_2$ mass flow | kg/h | | | | | | | | | | |
| HC mass flow | kg/h | | | | | | | | | | |
| $NO_x$ specific | g/kWh | | | | | | | | | | |

* As applicable.

Emissions test report no. ................ **Engine test data** Sheet 5/5

| **Mode** | | 1 | 2 | 3 | 4 | 5 | 6 | 7 | 8 | 9 | 10 |
|---|---|---|---|---|---|---|---|---|---|---|---|
| Power/torque | % | | | | | | | | | | |
| Speed | % | | | | | | | | | | |
| Time at beginning of mode | | | | | | | | | | | |
| **Engine data** | | | | | | | | | | | |
| Speed | rpm | | | | | | | | | | |
| Auxiliary power | kW | | | | | | | | | | |
| Dynamometer setting | kW | | | | | | | | | | |
| Power | kW | | | | | | | | | | |
| Mean effective pressure | kPa | | | | | | | | | | |
| Fuel rack | mm | | | | | | | | | | |
| Uncorrected spec. fuel consumption | g/kWh | | | | | | | | | | |
| Fuel flow | kg/h or $m^3/h$* | | | | | | | | | | |
| Air flow | kg/h | | | | | | | | | | |
| Exhaust flow ($q_{mew}$) | kg/h | | | | | | | | | | |
| Exhaust temperature | °C | | | | | | | | | | |
| Exhaust backpressure | kPa | | | | | | | | | | |
| Charge air coolant temperature in | °C | | | | | | | | | | |
| Charge air coolant temperature out | °C | | | | | | | | | | |
| Charge air temperature | °C | | | | | | | | | | |
| Charge air reference temperature | °C | | | | | | | | | | |
| Charge air pressure | kPa | | | | | | | | | | |
| Fuel oil temperature | °C | | | | | | | | | | |

* As applicable.

## Section 2 – Parent engine test data to be included in the technical file – see 2.4.1.5 of the Code

| Engine family/engine group reference | | |
|---|---|---|
| | | |
| **Parent engine** | | |
| Model/type | | |
| Nominated rated power | kW | |
| Nominated rated speed | rpm | |
| **Parent engine test fuel oil** | | |
| Reference fuel designation | | |
| ISO 8217:2005 grade (DM or RM) | | |
| Carbon | % m/m | |
| Hydrogen | % m/m | |
| Sulphur | % m/m | |
| Nitrogen | % m/m | |
| Oxygen | % m/m | |
| Water | % V/V | |

| Measured data (parent engine) | | | | | | | | | |
|---|---|---|---|---|---|---|---|---|---|
| Power/torque | % | | | | | | | | |
| Speed | % | | | | | | | | |
| Mode point | | 1 | 2 | 3 | 4 | 5 | 6 | 7 | 8 |
| **Engine Performance** | | | | | | | | | |
| Power | kW | | | | | | | | |
| Speed | rpm | | | | | | | | |
| Fuel flow | kg/h | | | | | | | | |
| Intake air flow (wet/dry) | kg/h | | | | | | | | |
| Exhaust gas flow | kg/h | | | | | | | | |
| Intake air temperature | °C | | | | | | | | |
| Charge air temperature | °C | | | | | | | | |
| Charge air reference temperature | °C | | | | | | | | |
| Charge air pressure | kPa | | | | | | | | |
| Additional parameter(s) used for emission corrections (specify) | | | | | | | | | |
| **Ambient conditions** | | | | | | | | | |
| Atmospheric pressure | kPa | | | | | | | | |
| Relative humidity (RH) of intake air | % | | | | | | | | |
| Air temperature at RH sensor* | °C | | | | | | | | |

* As applicable.

| | | | | | | | | | |
|---|---|---|---|---|---|---|---|---|---|
| Dry bulb temperature of intake air* | °C | | | | | | | | |
| Wet bulb temperature of intake air* | °C | | | | | | | | |
| Absolute humidity of intake air* | g/kg | | | | | | | | |
| **Emission concentrations** | | | | | | | | | |
| $NO_x$ wet/dry | ppm | | | | | | | | |
| $CO_2$ | % | | | | | | | | |
| $O_2$ wet/dry | % | | | | | | | | |
| CO | ppm | | | | | | | | |
| HC | ppmC | | | | | | | | |
| **Calculated data (parent engine)** | | | | | | | | | |
| Intake air humidity | g/kg | | | | | | | | |
| Charge air humidity | g/kg | | | | | | | | |
| Test condition parameter, $f_a$ | | | | | | | | | |
| Dry/wet correction factor, $k_{wr}$ | | | | | | | | | |
| $NO_x$ humidity correction factor, $k_{hd}$ | | | | | | | | | |
| Exhaust gas flow rate | kg/h | | | | | | | | |
| $NO_x$ emission flow rate | kg/h | | | | | | | | |
| Additional emission correction factor(s) (specify) | g/kWh | | | | | | | | |
| $NO_x$ emission | g/kWh | | | | | | | | |
| **Test cycle** | | | | | | | | | |
| **Emission value** | **g/kWh** | | | | | | | | |

* As applicable.

# *Appendix VI*

## Calculation of exhaust gas mass flow (carbon balance method)

*(Refer to chapter 5 of the $NO_x$ Technical Code 2008)*

### 1 Introduction

**1.1** This appendix addresses the calculation of the exhaust gas mass flow based on exhaust gas concentration measurement, and on the knowledge of fuel consumption. Symbols and descriptions of terms and variables used in the formulae for the carbon balance measurement method are summarized in the introduction of this Code.

**1.2** Except as otherwise specified, all results of calculations required by this appendix shall be reported in the engine's test report in accordance with 5.10 of this Code.

### 2 Carbon balance method, 1-step calculation procedure

**2.1** This method involves exhaust mass calculation from fuel consumption, fuel composition and exhaust gas concentrations.

**2.2** Exhaust gas mass flow rate on wet basis:

$$q_{mew} = q_{mf} \cdot \left( \left( \frac{1.4 \cdot (w_{BET} \cdot w_{BET})}{\frac{\left( \frac{(1.4 \cdot w_{BET})}{f_c} + (w_{ALF} \cdot 0.08936) - 1 \right) \frac{1}{1.293} + f_{fd}}{f_c \cdot f_c}} + (w_{ALF} \cdot 0.08936) - 1 \right) \cdot \left( 1 + \frac{H_a}{1000} \right) + 1 \right) \quad (1)$$

with:

$f_{fd}$ according to equation (2), $f_c$ according to equation (3).

$H_a$ is the absolute humidity of intake air, in gram water per kg dry air. However, if $H_a \geq H_{SC}$, then $H_{SC}$ shall be used in place of $H_a$ in formula (1).

*Note:* $H_a$ may be derived from relative humidity measurement, dew point measurement, vapour pressure measurement or dry/wet bulb measurement using the generally accepted formulae.

**2.3** The fuel-specific constant $f_{fd}$ for the dry exhaust shall be calculated by adding up the additional volumes of the combustion of the fuel elements:

$$f_{fd} = -0.055593 \cdot w_{ALF} + 0.008002 \cdot w_{DEL} + 0.0070046 \cdot w_{EPS} \quad (2)$$

**2.4** Carbon factor $f_c$ according to equation (3):

$$f_c = (c_{CO2d} - c_{CO2ad}) \cdot 0.5441 + \frac{c_{COd}}{18522} + \frac{c_{HCw}}{17355} \quad (3)$$

with

$c_{CO2d}$ = dry $CO_2$ concentration in the raw exhaust, %

$c_{CO2ad}$ = dry $CO_2$ concentration in the ambient air, % = 0.03%

$c_{COd}$ = dry CO concentration in the raw exhaust, ppm

$c_{HCw}$ = wet HC concentration in the raw exhaust, ppm

# *Appendix VII*

## Checklist for an engine parameter check method

*(Refer to 6.2.2.5 of the $NO_x$ Technical Code 2008)*

**1** For some of the parameters listed below, more than one survey possibility exists. In such cases, as a guideline, any one of, or a combination of, the below-listed methods may be sufficient to show compliance. As approved by the Administration, the shipowner, supported by the applicant for engine certification, may choose which method is applicable.

**.1** parameter "injection timing":

**.1** Fuel cam position (individual cam or camshaft if cams are not adjustable):

- optional (dependent on design): position of a link between the cam and the pump drive,
- optional for sleeve-metered pumps: variable injection timing (VIT) index and cam position or position of the barrel, or
- other sleeve-metering device;

**.2** start of delivery for certain fuel rack positions (dynamic pressure measurement);

**.3** opening of injection valve for certain load points, e.g., using a Hall sensor or acceleration pick-up;

**.4** load-dependent operating values for charge air pressure, combustion peak pressure, charge air temperature, exhaust gas temperature versus graphs showing the correlation with $NO_x$. Additionally, it shall be ensured that the compression ratio corresponds to the initial certification value (see 1.7).

*Note:* To assess the actual timing, it is necessary to know the allowable limits for meeting the emission limits or even graphs showing the influence of timing on $NO_x$, based on the test-bed measurement results.

**.2** parameter "injection nozzle":

**.1** specification and component identification number;

**.3** parameter "injection pump":

- **.1** component identification number (specifying plunger and barrel design);

**.4** parameter "fuel cam":

- **.1** component identification number (specifying shape);
- **.2** start and end of delivery for a certain fuel rack position (dynamic pressure measurement);

**.5** parameter "injection pressure":

- **.1** only for common-rail systems: load-dependent pressure in the rail, graph showing correlation with $NO_x$;

**.6** parameter "combustion chamber":

- **.1** component identification numbers for the cylinder head and piston head;

**.7** parameter "compression ratio":

- **.1** check for actual clearance;
- **.2** check for shims in piston rod or connecting rod;

**.8** parameter "turbocharger type and build":

- **.1** model and specification (identification numbers);
- **.2** load-dependent charge air pressure, graph showing the correlation with $NO_x$;

**.9** parameter "charge air cooler, charge air heater":

- **.1** model and specification;
- **.2** load-dependent charge air temperature corrected to reference conditions, graph showing the correlation with $NO_x$;

**.10** parameter "valve timing" (only for 4-stroke engines with inlet valve closure before bottom dead centre (BDC)):

- **.1** cam position;
- **.2** check actual timing;

**.11** parameter "water injection" (for assessment: graph showing influence on $NO_x$):

- **.1** load-dependent water consumption (monitoring);

**.12** parameter "emulsified fuel" (for assessment: graph showing influence on $NO_x$):

- **.1** load-dependent fuel rack position (monitoring);
- **.2** load-dependent water consumption (monitoring);

**.13** parameter "exhaust gas recirculation" (for assessment: graph showing influence on $NO_x$):

- **.1** load-dependent mass flow of recirculated exhaust gas (monitoring);
- **.2** $CO_2$ concentration in the mixture of fresh air and recirculated exhaust gas, i.e., in the "scavenge air" (monitoring);
- **.3** $O_2$ concentration in the "scavenge air" (monitoring);

**.14** parameter "selective catalytic reduction" (SCR):

- **.1** load-dependent mass flow of reducing agent (monitoring) and additional periodical spot checks on $NO_x$ concentration after SCR (for assessment: graph showing influence on $NO_x$).

**2** For engines with selective catalytic reduction (SCR) without feedback control, optional $NO_x$ measurement (periodical spot checks or monitoring) is useful to show that the SCR efficiency still corresponds to the state at the time of certification regardless of whether the ambient conditions or the fuel quality has led to different raw emissions.

# *Appendix VIII*

## Implementation of the direct measurement and monitoring method

*(Refer to 6.4 of the $NO_x$ Technical Code 2008)*

### 1 Electrical equipment: materials and design

**1.1** Electrical equipment shall be constructed of durable, flame-retardant, moisture-resistant materials that are not subject to deterioration in the installed environment and at the temperatures to which the equipment is likely to be exposed.

**1.2** Electrical equipment shall be designed such that current-carrying parts with potential to earth are protected against accidental contact.

### 2 Analysing equipment

**2.1** *Analysers*

**2.1.1** The exhaust gases shall be analysed with the following instruments. For non-linear analysers, the use of linearizing circuits is permitted. Other systems or analysers may be accepted, subject to the approval of the Administration, provided they yield equivalent results to that of the equipment referenced below:

**.1** Nitrogen oxides ($NO_x$) analysis

The nitrogen oxides analyser shall be of the chemiluminescent detector (CLD) or heated chemiluminescent detector (HCLD) type. The exhaust gas sampled for $NO_x$ measurement shall be maintained above its dew point temperature until it has passed through the $NO_2$-to-NO converter.

*Note:* In the case of raw exhaust gas this temperature shall be greater than 60°C if the engine is fuelled with ISO 8217:2005 DM-grade type fuel and greater than 140°C if fuelled with ISO 8217:2005 RM-grade type fuel.

**.2** Carbon dioxide ($CO_2$) analysis

When required, the carbon dioxide analyser shall be of the non-dispersive infrared (NDIR) absorption type.

**.3** Carbon monoxide (CO) analysis

When required, the carbon monoxide analyser shall be of the NDIR absorption type.

**.4** Hydrocarbon (HC) analysis

When required, the hydrocarbon analyser shall be of the heated flame ionization detector (HFID) type. The exhaust gas sampled for HC measurement shall be maintained at 190°C ± 10°C from the sample point to the detector.

**.5** Oxygen ($O_2$) analysis

When required, the oxygen analyser shall be of the paramagnetic detector (PMD), zirconium dioxide (ZRDO) or electrochemical sensor (ECS) type.

**2.2** *Analyser specifications*

**2.2.1** The analyser specifications shall be consistent with 1.6, 1.7, 1.8, 1.9 and 1.10 of appendix III of this Code.

**2.2.2** The analyser range shall be such that the measured emission value is within 15% – 100% of the range used.

**2.2.3** The analysing equipment shall be installed and maintained in accordance with manufacturers' recommendations in order to meet the requirements of 1.7, 1.8, 1.9, and 1.10 of appendix III of this Code and sections 7 and 9 of appendix IV of this Code.

## 3 Pure and calibration gases

**3.1** Pure and calibration gases, as required, shall comply with 2.1 and 2.2 of appendix IV of this Code. Declared concentrations shall be traceable to national and/or international standards. Calibration gases shall be in accordance with the analysing equipment manufacturers' recommendations.

**3.2** Analyser span gases shall be between 80% – 100% of the analyser scale being spanned.

## 4 Gas sampling and transfer system

**4.1** The exhaust gas sample shall be representative of the average exhaust emission from all the engine's cylinders. The gas sampling system shall comply with 5.9.3 of this Code.

**4.2** The exhaust gas sample shall be drawn from a zone within 10% to 90% of the duct diameter.

**4.3** In order to facilitate the installation of the sampling probe, an example of a sample point connection flange is given in section 5.

**4.4** The exhaust gas sample for $NO_x$ measurement shall be maintained so as to prevent $NO_2$ loss via water or acid condensation in accordance with analysing equipment manufacturers' recommendations.

**4.5** The gas sample shall not be dried by chemical dryers.

**4.6** The gas sampling system shall be capable of being verified to be free of ingress leakage in accordance with analysing equipment manufacturers' recommendations.

**4.7** An additional sample point adjacent to that used shall be provided to facilitate quality control checks on the system.

## 5 Sample point connection flange

**5.1** The following is an example of a general purpose sample point connection flange, which shall be sited, as convenient, on the exhaust duct of each engine for which it may be required to demonstrate compliance by means of the direct measurement and monitoring method.

| Description | Dimension |
|---|---|
| Outer diameter | 160 mm |
| Inner diameter | 35 mm |
| Flange thickness | 9 mm |
| Bolt circle diameter 1 | 130 mm |
| Bolt circle diameter 2 | 65 mm |
| Flange slots | 4 holes, each 12 mm diameter, equidistantly placed on each of the above bolt circle diameters. Holes on the two bolt circle diameters to be aligned on same radii. Flange to be slotted, 12 mm wide, between inner and outer bolt circle diameter holes. |
| Bolts and nuts | 4 sets, diameter and length as required. |
| Flange shall be of steel and be finished with a flat face. | |

**5.2** The flange shall be fitted to a stub pipe of suitable gauge material aligned with the exhaust duct diameter. The stub pipe shall be no longer than necessary to project beyond the exhaust duct cladding, sufficient to enable access to the far side of the flange. The stub pipe shall be insulated. The stub pipe shall terminate at an accessible position free from nearby obstructions that would interfere with the location or mounting of a sample probe and associated fittings.

**5.3** When not in use, the stub pipe shall be closed with a steel blank flange and a gasket of suitable heat-resisting material. The sampling flange, and closing blank flange, when not in use, shall be covered with a readily removable and suitable heat-resistant material that protects against accidental contact.

## 6 Selection of load points and revised weighting factors

**6.1** As provided for by 6.4.6.4 of this Code, in the case of the E2, E3 or D2 test cycles, the minimum number of load points shall be such that the combined nominal weighting factors, as given in 3.2 of this Code, are greater than 0.5.

**6.2** In accordance with 6.1, for the E2 and E3 test cycles it would be necessary to use the 75% load point plus one or more other load points. In the case of the D2 test cycle, either the 25% or 50% load point shall be used plus either one or more load points such that the combined nominal weighting factor is greater than 0.5.

**6.3** The examples below give some of the possible combinations of load points that may be used together with the respective revised weighting factors:

**.1** E2 and E3 test cycles

| **Power** | **100%** | **75%** | **50%** | **25%** |
|---|---|---|---|---|
| Nominal weighting factor | 0.2 | 0.5 | 0.15 | 0.15 |
| Option A | 0.29 | 0.71 | | |
| Option B | | 0.77 | 0.23 | |
| Option C | 0.24 | 0.59 | | 0.18 |
| Plus other combinations that result in a combined nominal weighting factor greater than 0.5. Hence use of the 100% + 50% + 25% load points would be insufficient. | | | | |

**.2** D2 test cycle

| **Power** | **100%** | **75%** | **50%** | **25%** | **10%** |
|---|---|---|---|---|---|
| Nominal weighting factor | 0.05 | 0.25 | 0.3 | 0.3 | 0.1 |
| Option D | | | 0.5 | 0.5 | |
| Option E | | 0.45 | | 0.55 | |
| Option F | | 0.38 | 0.46 | | 0.15 |
| Option G | 0.06 | 0.28 | 0.33 | 0.33 | |
| Plus other combinations that result in a combined nominal weighting factor greater than 0.5. Hence use of the 100% + 50% + 10% load points would be insufficient. | | | | | |

**6.4** In the case of the C1 test cycle, as a minimum, one load point from each of the rated, intermediate and idle speed sections shall be used. The examples below give some of the possible combinations of load points that may be used together with the respective revised weighting factors:

**.1** C1 test cycle

| **Speed** | **Rated** | | | | **Intermediate** | | | **Idle** |
|---|---|---|---|---|---|---|---|---|
| Torque | 100% | 75% | 50% | 10% | 100% | 75% | 50% | 0% |
| Nominal weighting factor | 0.15 | 0.15 | 0.15 | 0.1 | 0.1 | 0.1 | 0.1 | 0.15 |
| Option H | | 0.38 | | | 0.25 | | | 0.38 |
| Option I | | | | 0.29 | | 0.29 | | 0.43 |
| Option J | 0.27 | 0.27 | | | | | 0.18 | 0.27 |
| Option K | 0.19 | 0.19 | 0.19 | 0.13 | | 0.13 | | 0.19 |
| Plus other combinations incorporating at least one load point at each of rated, intermediate and idle speeds. | | | | | | | | |

**6.5** Examples of calculation of revised weighting factors:

**.1** For a given load point, revised weighting factors shall be calculated as follows:

y% load = nominal weighting factor at load y · (1/(sum of the load factors for load points where data were acquired))

**.2** For Option A:

75% load: revised value is calculated as: $0.5 \cdot (1/(0.5 + 0.2)) = 0.71$

100% load: revised value is calculated as: $0.2 \cdot (1/(0.5 + 0.2)) = 0.29$

**.3** For Option F:

75% load: revised value is calculated as: $0.25 \cdot (1/(0.25 + 0.3 + 0.1)) = 0.38$

**.4** The revised weighting factors are shown to two decimal places. However, the values to be applied to equation (19) of this Code shall be to the full precision. Hence in the Option F case above the revised weighting factor is shown as 0.38 although the actual calculated value is 0.384615... . Consequently, in these examples of revised weighting factors the summation of the values shown (to two decimal places) may not sum to 1.00 due to rounding.

## 7 Determination of power set point stability

**7.1** To determine set point stability, the power coefficient of variance shall be calculated over a 10-minute interval, and the sampling rate shall be at least 1 Hz. The result shall be less than or equal to five per cent (5%).

**7.2** The formulae for calculating the coefficient of variance are as follows:

$$Ave = \frac{1}{N}\sum_{j=1}^{N} x_j \tag{1}$$

$$S.D. = \sqrt{\frac{1}{N-1}\sum_{i=1}^{N}(x_i - Ave)^2} \tag{2}$$

$$\%C.O.V. = \frac{S.D.}{Ave} \cdot 100 \leq 5\% \tag{3}$$

where:

$\%C.O.V.$ = power coefficient of variance in %

$S.D.$ = standard deviation

$Ave$ = average

$N$ = total number of data points sampled
$x_i, x_j$ = $i^{\text{th}}$, $j^{\text{th}}$ value of power data point in kW
$i$ = index variable in standard deviation formula
$j$ = index variable in average formula.

# ADDITIONAL INFORMATION

## MEPC.1/Circ.638

*17 November 2008*

# INTERIM GUIDELINES FOR THE APPLICATION OF THE $NO_x$ TECHNICAL CODE 2008

**1** The Marine Environment Protection Committee, at its fifty-eighth session (6 to 10 October 2008), adopted, by resolution MEPC.176(58), a revised MARPOL Annex VI and by resolution MEPC.177(58), a revised Technical Code on Control of Emission of Nitrogen Oxides from Marine Diesel Engines ($NO_x$ Technical Code 2008).

**2** The purpose of the $NO_x$ Technical Code 2008 is to provide mandatory procedures for the testing, survey and certification of marine diesel engines to ensure that they comply with the standards set forth in regulation 13 of the revised MARPOL Annex VI. These procedures will enable engine manufacturers, shipowners, and Administrations to comply with regulation 13 of the revised MARPOL Annex VI.

**3** The requirements of regulation 13 of the revised MARPOL Annex VI specifically include regulations for Tier II $NO_x$ requirements, which are to become effective in respect of ships constructed on or after 1 January 2011. Since the revised MARPOL Annex VI is set to enter into force on 1 July 2010, there is a period of only six months for Administrations to certify engines and issue Engine International Air Pollution Prevention (EIAPP) Certificates, in order to comply with regulation 13.4.

**4** With a view to alleviating possible implementation difficulties posed by the six-month period between the entry-into-force date of the revised MARPOL Annex VI and the effective date for Tier II compliance, Administrations are invited to apply the procedures in the $NO_x$ Technical Code 2008 prior to the entry-into-force date of the revised MARPOL Annex VI by using the interim guidelines as set out in the annex to this circular.

## Annex

### *Interim Guidelines for the application of the $NO_x$ Technical Code 2008*

**1** Each engine, which will become subject to the provisions of regulation 13.4 of the revised MARPOL Annex VI upon its entry into force, should be certified in accordance with the requirements of the $NO_x$ Technical Code 2008.

**2** Pending entry into force of the revised MARPOL Annex VI and upon satisfactory demonstration of compliance with the $NO_x$ Technical Code 2008 requirements, a "Statement of Compliance" with the $NO_x$ Technical Code 2008 should be issued by the Administration or an organization acting on behalf of that Administration. Such a Statement of Compliance should contain as a minimum the information required by appendix 1 of the $NO_x$ Technical Code 2008.

**3** The Statement of Compliance is intended as an interim measure pending issuance of the Engine International Air Pollution Prevention (EIAPP) Certificates upon entry into force of the $NO_x$ Technical Code 2008.

**4** Administrations are urged to take into consideration the Statement of Compliance when issuing EIAPP Certificates in accordance with the $NO_x$ Technical Code 2008, whether or not the Statement of Compliance was issued by the Administration, or an organization acting on behalf of that Administration, or by another Government.

## Resolution MEPC.76(40)

*(adopted on 25 September 1997)*
*as amended by resolution MEPC.93(45)*

# STANDARD SPECIFICATION FOR SHIPBOARD INCINERATORS

THE MARINE ENVIRONMENT PROTECTION COMMITTEE,

RECALLING Article 38(c) of the Convention on the International Maritime Organization concerning the function of the Committee,

RECALLING ALSO that Annex V of the International Convention for the Prevention of Pollution from Ships, 1973, as modified by the Protocol of 1978 relating thereto (MARPOL 73/78), provides regulations for the prevention of pollution by garbage from ships,

RECOGNIZING that the Assembly at its seventeenth session adopted resolution A.719(17) on prevention of air pollution from ships, and requested the Committee and the Maritime Safety Committee to develop environmentally based standards for incineration of garbage and other ship-generated waste,

RECOGNIZING ALSO that the Committee, at its thirty-third session, adopted resolution MEPC.59(33) – Revised Guidelines for the Implementation of Annex V of MARPOL 73/78, which included the original text of the Standard Specification for Shipboard Incinerators,

NOTING that the Conference of Parties to MARPOL 73/78, held in conjunction with MEPC 40, adopted the Protocol of 1997 to amend MARPOL 73/78, including its Annex VI – Regulations for the Prevention of Air Pollution from Ships,

BEING AWARE that the regulation 16(2) on shipboard incinerators within Annex VI to MARPOL 73/78 includes reference to mandatory operating limits for shipboard incinerators as contained in appendix IV to Annex VI and approval of such incinerators by the Administration to be based on the standard specification developed by the Organization,

ALSO BEING AWARE that regulation 16 of Annex VI of MARPOL 73/78 prohibits shipboard incineration of certain substances,

HAVING CONSIDERED the recommendations by the Sub-Committee on Ship Design and Equipment at its fortieth session regarding the Standard Specification for Shipboard Incinerators,

1. ADOPTS the Standard Specification for Shipboard Incinerators, the text of which supersedes Appendix 2 to the Revised Guidelines for the Implementation of Annex V of MARPOL 73/78, adopted by resolution MEPC.59(33), and which is set out at Annex to this resolution; and

2. URGES Governments to apply the Standard Specification for Shipboard Incinerators when implementing the provisions of Annexes V and VI of MARPOL 73/78.

# Annex

*Standard specification for shipboard incinerators*

## Contents

## 1 Scope

**1.1** This specification covers the design, manufacture, performance, operation and testing of incinerators intended to incinerate garbage and other shipboard wastes generated during the ship's normal service.

**1.2** This specification applies to those incinerator plants with capacities up to 1,500 kW per unit.

**1.3** This specification does not apply to systems on special incinerator ships, e.g., for burning industrial wastes such as chemicals, manufacturing residues, etc.

**1.4** This specification does not address the electrical supply to the unit, nor the foundation connections and stack connections.

**1.5** This specification provides emission requirements in annex A1, and fire protection requirements in annex A2. Provisions for incinerators integrated with heat recovery units and provisions for flue gas temperature are given in annex A3 and annex A4, respectively.

**1.6** This specification may involve hazardous materials, operations, and equipment. This standard does not purport to address all of the safety problems associated with its use. It is the responsibility of the user of this standard to establish appropriate safety and health practices and determine the applicability of regulatory limitations prior to use, including possible port State limitations.

## 2 Definitions

**2.1** *Ship* means a vessel of any type whatsoever operating in the marine environment and includes hydrofoil boats, air-cushioned vehicles, submersibles, floating craft and fixed or floating platforms.

**2.2** *Incinerator* means shipboard facilities for incinerating solid wastes approximating in composition to household waste and liquid wastes arising from the operation of the ship, e.g., domestic waste, cargo-associated waste, maintenance waste, operational waste, cargo residues, and fishing gear, etc. These facilities may be designed to use or not to use the heat energy produced.

**2.3** *Garbage* means all kinds of victual, domestic and operational waste excluding fresh fish and parts thereof, generated during normal operation of the ship as defined in Annex V to MARPOL 73/78.

**2.4** *Waste* means useless, unneeded or superfluous matter which is to be discarded.

**2.5** *Food wastes* are any spoiled or unspoiled victual substances, such as fruits, vegetables, dairy products, poultry, meat products, food scraps, food particles, and all other materials contaminated by such wastes, generated aboard ship, principally in the galley and dining areas.

**2.6** *Plastic* means a solid material which contains as an essential ingredient one or more synthetic organic high polymers and which is formed (shaped) during either manufacture of the polymer or the fabrication into a finished product by heat and/or pressure. Plastics have material properties ranging from hard and brittle to soft and elastic. Plastics are used for a variety of marine purposes including, but not limited to, packaging (vapour-proof barriers, bottles, containers, liners), ship construction (fibreglass and laminated structures, siding, piping, insulation, flooring, carpets, fabrics, paints and finishes, adhesives, electrical and electronic components), disposable eating utensils and cups, bags, sheeting, floats, fishing nets, strapping bands, rope and line.

**2.7** *Domestic waste* means all types of food wastes, sewage and wastes generated in the living spaces on board the ship for the purpose of this specification.

**2.8** *Cargo-associated waste* means all materials which have become wastes as a result of use on board a ship for cargo stowage and handling. Cargo-associated waste includes but is not limited to dunnage, shoring pallets, lining and packing materials, plywood, paper, cardboard, wire, and steel strapping.

**2.9** *Maintenance waste* means materials collected by the engine department and the deck department while maintaining and operating the vessel, such as soot, machinery deposits, scraped paint, deck sweeping, wiping wastes, oily rags, etc.

**2.10** *Operational wastes* means all cargo-associated wastes and maintenance waste (including ash and clinkers), and cargo residues defined as garbage in 2.13.

**2.11** *Sludge oil* means sludge from fuel and lubricating oil separators, waste lubricating oil from main and auxiliary machinery, waste oil from bilge water separators, drip trays, etc.

**2.12** *Oily rags* are rags which have been saturated with oil as controlled in Annex I to the Convention. Contaminated rags are rags which have been saturated with a substance defined as a harmful substance in the other Annexes to MARPOL 73/78.

**2.13** *Cargo residues* for the purposes of this standard are defined as the remnants of any cargo material on board that cannot be placed in proper cargo holds (loading excess and spillage) or which remains in cargo holds and elsewhere after unloading procedures are completed (unloading residual and spillage). However, cargo residues are expected to be in small quantities.

**2.14** *Fishing gear* is defined as any physical device or part thereof or combination of items that may be placed on or in the water with the intended purpose of capturing, or controlling for subsequent capture, living marine or freshwater organisms.

## 3 Materials and manufacture

**3.1** The materials used in the individual parts of the incinerator are to be suitable for the intended application with respect to heat resistance, mechanical properties, oxidation, corrosion, etc., as in other auxiliary marine equipment.

**3.2** Piping for fuel and sludge oil should be seamless steel of adequate strength and to the satisfaction of the Administration. Short lengths of steel, or annealed copper nickel, nickel copper, or copper pipe and tubing may be used at the burners. The use of nonmetallic materials for fuel lines is prohibited. Valves and fittings may be threaded in sizes up to and including 60 mm O.D. (outside diameter), but threaded unions are not to be used on pressure lines in sizes 33 mm O.D. (outside diameter) and over.

**3.3** All rotating or moving mechanical and exposed electrical parts should be protected against accidental contact.

**3.4** Incinerator walls are to be protected with insulated fire bricks/ refractory and a cooling system. Outside surface temperature of the incinerator casing being touched during normal operations should not exceed 20°C above ambient temperature.

**3.5** Refractory should be resistant to thermal shocks and resistant to normal ship's vibration. The refractory design temperature should be equal to the combustion chamber design temperature plus 20%. (See 4.1.)

**3.6** Incinerating systems should be designed such that corrosion will be minimized on the inside of the systems.

**3.7** In systems equipped for incinerating liquid wastes, safe ignition and maintenance of combustion must be ensured, e.g., by a supplementary burner using gas oil/diesel oil or equivalent.

**3.8** The combustion chamber(s) should be designed for easy maintenance of all internal parts including the refractory and insulation.

**3.9** The combustion process should take place under negative pressure which means that the pressure in the furnace under all circumstances should be lower than the ambient pressure in the room where the incinerator is installed. A flue gas fan may be fitted to secure negative pressure.

**3.10** The incinerating furnace may be charged with solid waste either by hand or automatically. In every case, fire dangers should be avoided and charging should be possible without danger to the operating personnel.

For instance, where charging is carried out by hand, a charging lock may be provided which ensures that the charging space is isolated from the fire box as long as the filling hatch is open.

Where charging is not effected through a charging lock, an interlock should be installed to prevent the charging door from opening while the incinerator is in operation with burning of garbage in progress or while the furnace temperature is above 220°C.

**3.11** Incinerators equipped with a feeding sluice or system should ensure that the material charged will move to the combustion chamber. Such system should be designed such that both operator and environment are protected from hazardous exposure.

**3.12** Interlocks should be installed to prevent ash removal doors from opening while burning is in progress or while the furnace temperature is above 220°C.

**3.13** The incinerator should be provided with a safe observation port of the combustion chamber in order to provide visual control of the burning process and waste accumulation in the combustion chamber. Neither heat, flame, nor particles should be able to pass through the observation port. An example of a safe observation port is high-temperature glass with a metal closure.

**3.14** *Electrical requirements*[*]

**3.14.1** Electrical installation requirements should apply to all electrical equipment, including controls, safety devices, cables, and burners and incinerators.

**3.14.1.1** A disconnecting means capable of being locked in the open position should be installed at an accessible location at the incinerator so that the incinerator can be disconnected from all sources of potential. This disconnecting means should be an integral part of the incinerator or adjacent to it. (See 5.1.)

**3.14.1.2** All uninsulated live metal parts should be guarded to avoid accidental contact.

**3.14.1.3** The electrical equipment should be so arranged so that failure of this equipment will cause the fuel supply to be shut off.

**3.14.1.4** All electrical contacts of every safety device installed in the control circuit should be electrically connected in series. However, special consideration should be given to arrangements when certain devices are wired in parallel.

**3.14.1.5** All electrical components and devices should have a voltage rating commensurate with the supply voltage of the control system.

**3.14.1.6** All electrical devices and electric equipment exposed to the weather should meet the requirements of international standards acceptable to the Organization.[†]

**3.14.1.7** All electrical and mechanical control devices should be of a type tested and accepted by a nationally recognized testing agency, according to international standards.

**3.14.1.8** The design of the control circuits should be such that limit and primary safety controls should directly open a circuit that functions to interrupt the supply of fuel to combustion units.

---

[*] International Electrotechnical Commission (IEC) Standards, particularly IEC Publication 92 – Electrical Installations in Ships and Mobile and Fixed Offshore Units, are applicable for this equipment.

[†] Refer to IEC Publication 92-201, Table V (1980 edition).

**3.14.2** Overcurrent protection

**3.14.2.1** Conductors for interconnecting wiring that is smaller than the supply conductors should be provided with overcurrent protection based on the size of the smallest interconnecting conductors external to any control box, in accordance with the requirements of international standards acceptable to the Organization.*

**3.14.2.2** Overcurrent protection for interconnecting wiring should be located at the point where the smaller conductors connect to the larger conductors. However, overall overcurrent protection is acceptable if it is sized on the basis of the smallest conductors of the interconnecting wiring, or in accordance with the requirements of international standards acceptable to the Organization.*

**3.14.2.3** Overcurrent protection devices should be accessible and their function should be identified.

**3.14.3** Motors

**3.14.3.1** All electric motors should have enclosures corresponding to the environment where they are located, at least IP 44, in accordance with the requirements of international standards acceptable to the Organization.†

**3.14.3.2** Motors should be provided with a corrosion-resistant name-plate specifying information in accordance with the requirements of international standards acceptable to the Organization.‡

**3.14.3.3** Motors should be provided with running protection by means of integral thermal protection, by overcurrent devices, or a combination of both in accordance with manufacturer's instruction that should meet the requirements of international standards acceptable to the Organization.*

**3.14.3.4** Motors should be rated for continuous duty and should be designed for an ambient temperature of 45°C or higher.

**3.14.3.5** All motors should be provided with terminal leads or terminal screws in terminal boxes integral with, or secured to, the motor frames.

* Refer to IEC Publication 92-202 (1980 edition with amendment).

† Refer to IEC Publication 529 (1976 edition with amendment).

‡ Refer to IEC Publication 92-301 (1980 edition).

**3.14.4** Ignition system

**3.14.4.1** When automatic electric ignition is provided, it should be accomplished by means of either a high-voltage electric spark, a high-energy electric spark, or a glow coil.

**3.14.4.2** Ignition transformers should have an enclosure corresponding to the environment where they are located, at least IP 44 in accordance with the requirements of international standards acceptable to the Organization.*

**3.14.4.3** Ignition cable should meet the requirements of international standards acceptable to the Organization.†

**3.14.5** Wiring

**3.14.5.1** All wiring for incinerators should be rated and selected in accordance with the requirements of international standards acceptable to the Organization.‡

**3.14.6** Bonding and grounding

**3.14.6.1** Means should be provided for grounding the major metallic frame or assembly of the incinerators.

**3.14.6.2** Noncurrent carrying enclosures, frames and similar parts of all electrical components and devices should be bonded to the main frame or assembly of the incinerator. Electrical components that are bonded by their installation do not require a separate bonding conductor.

**3.14.6.3** When an insulated conductor is used to bond electrical components and devices, it should show a continuous green colour, with or without a yellow stripe.

## 4 Operating requirements

**4.1** The incinerator system should be designed and constructed for operation with the following conditions:

| | |
|---|---|
| Maximum combustion chamber flue gas outlet temperature | 1200°C |
| Minimum combustion chamber flue gas outlet temperature | 850°C |
| Preheat temperature of combustion chamber | 650°C |

---

* Refer to IEC Publication 529 (1976 edition with amendment).

† Refer to IEC Publication 92-503 (1975 edition).

‡ Refer to IEC Publication 92-352 (1979 edition with amendments).

For Batch Loaded Incinerators, there are no preheating requirements. However, the incinerator should be designed that the temperature in the actual combustion space should reach 600°C within 5 minutes after start.

| | |
|---|---|
| Prepurge, before ignition: | at least 4 air changes in the chamber(s) and stack, but not less than 15 seconds. |
| Time between restarts: | at least 4 air changes in the chamber(s) and stack, but not less than 15 seconds. |
| Postpurge, after shut-off fuel oil: | not less than 15 seconds after the closing of the fuel oil valve. |
| Incinerator discharge gases: | Minimum 6% $O_2$ (measured in dry flue gas). |

**4.2** Outside surface of combustion chamber(s) should be shielded from contact such that people in normal work situations will not be exposed to extreme heat (20°C above ambient temperature) or direct contact of surface temperatures exceeding 60°C. Examples for alternatives to accomplish this are a double jacket with an air flow in between or an expanded metal jacket.

**4.3** Incinerating systems are to be operated with underpressure (negative pressure) in the combustion chamber such that no gases or smoke can leak out to the surrounding areas.

**4.4** The incinerator should have warning plates attached in a prominent location on the unit, warning against unauthorized opening of doors to combustion chamber(s) during operation and against overloading the incinerator with garbage.

**4.5** The incinerator should have instruction plate(s) attached in a prominent location on the unit that clearly addresses the following:

**4.5.1** Cleaning ashes and slag from the combustion chamber(s) and cleaning of combustion air openings before starting the incinerator (where applicable).

**4.5.2** Operating procedures and instructions. These should include proper start-up procedures, normal shut-down procedures, emergency shut-down procedures, and procedures for loading garbage (where applicable).

**4.6** To avoid building up of dioxins, the flue gas should be shock-cooled to a maximum 350°C within 2.5 metres from the combustion chamber flue gas outlet.

## 5 Operating controls

**5.1** The entire unit should be capable of being disconnected from all sources of electricity by means of one disconnect switch located near the incinerator. (See 3.14.1.1.)

**5.2** There should be an emergency stop switch located outside the compartment which stops all power to the equipment. The emergency stop switch should also be able to stop all power to the fuel pumps. If the incinerator is equipped with a flue gas fan, the fan should be capable of being restarted independently of the other equipment on the incinerator.

**5.3** The control equipment should be so designed that any failure of the following equipment will prevent continued operations and cause the fuel supply to be cut off.

**5.3.1** Safety thermostat/draft failure

**5.3.1.1** A flue gas temperature controller, with a sensor placed in the flue gas duct, should be provided that will shut down the burner if the flue gas temperature exceeds the temperature set by the manufacturer for the specific design.

**5.3.1.2** A combustion temperature controller, with a sensor placed in the combustion chamber, should be provided that will shut down the burner if the combustion chamber temperature exceeds the maximum temperature.

**5.3.1.3** A negative pressure switch should be provided to monitor the draft and the negative pressure in the combustion chamber. The purpose of this negative pressure switch is to ensure that there is sufficient draft/negative pressure in the incinerator during operations. The circuit to the program relay for the burner will be opened and an alarm activated before the negative pressure rises to atmospheric pressure.

**5.3.2** Flame failure/fuel oil pressure

**5.3.2.1** The incinerator should have a flame safeguard control consisting of a flame sensing element and associated equipment for shut down of the unit in the event of ignition failure and flame failure during the firing cycle. The flame safeguard control should be so designed that the failure of any component will cause a safety shut down.

**5.3.2.2** The flame safeguard control should be capable of closing the fuel valves in not more than 4 seconds after a flame failure.

**5.3.2.3** The flame safeguard control should provide a trial-for-ignition period of not more that 10 seconds during which fuel may be supplied to establish flame. If flame is not established within 10 seconds, the fuel supply to the burners should be immediately shut off automatically.

**5.3.2.4** Whenever the flame safeguard control has operated because of failure of ignition, flame failure, or failure of any component, only one automatic restart may be provided. If this is not successful then manual reset of the flame safeguard control should be required for restart.

**5.3.2.5** Flame safeguard controls of the thermostatic type, such as stack switches and pyrostats operated by means of an open bimetallic helix, are prohibited.

**5.3.2.6** If fuel oil pressure drops below that set by the manufacturer, a failure and lock out of the program relay should result. This also applies to a sludge oil burner. (Applies where pressure is important for the combustion process or a pump is not an integral part of the burner.)

**5.3.3** Loss of power

If there is a loss of power to the incinerator control/alarm panel (not remote alarm panel), the system should shut down.

### 5.4 *Fuel supply*

Two fuel control solenoid valves should be provided in series in the fuel supply line to each burner. On multiple burner units, a valve on the main fuel supply line and a valve at each burner will satisfy this requirement. The valves should be connected electrically in parallel so that both operate simultaneously.

### 5.5 *Alarms*

**5.5.1** An outlet for an audible alarm should be provided for connection to a local alarm system or a central alarm system. When a failure occurs, a visible indicator should show what caused the failure. (The indicator may cover more than one fault condition.)

**5.5.2** The visible indicators should be designed so that, where failure is a safety related shutdown, manual reset is required.

**5.6** After shutdown of the oil burner, provision should be made for the fire box to cool sufficiently. (As an example of how this may be accomplished, the exhaust fan or ejector could be designed to continue to operate. This would not apply in the case of an emergency manual trip.)

## 6 Other requirements

### 6.1 *Documentation*

A complete instruction and maintenance manual with drawings, electric diagrams, spare parts list, etc., should be furnished with each incinerator.

### 6.2 *Installation*

All devices and components should, as fitted in the ship, be designed to operate when the ship is upright and when inclined at any angle of list up to and including 15° either way under static conditions and 22.5° under dynamic conditions (rolling) either way and simultaneously inclined dynamically (pitching) 7.5° by bow or stern.

### 6.3 *Incinerator*

**6.3.1** Incinerators are to be fitted with an energy source with sufficient energy to ensure a safe ignition and complete combustion. The combustion is to take place at sufficient negative pressure in the combustion chamber(s) to ensure no gases or smoke leaking out to the surrounding areas. (See 5.3.1.3.)

**6.3.2** A driptray is to be fitted under each burner and under any pumps, strainers, etc., that require occasional examination.

## 7 Tests

### 7.1 *Prototype tests*

An operating test for the prototype of each design should be conducted, with a test report completed indicating results of all tests. The tests should be conducted to ensure that all of the control components have been properly installed and that all parts of the incinerator, including controls and safety devices, are in satisfactory operating condition. Tests should include those described in section 7.3 below.

### **7.2** *Factory tests*

For each unit, if preassembled, an operating test should be conducted to ensure that all of the control components have been properly installed and that all parts of the incinerator, including controls and safety devices, are in satisfactory operating condition. Tests should include those described in 7.3 below.

### **7.3** *Installation tests*

An operating test after installation should be conducted to ensure that all of the control components have been properly installed and that all parts of the incinerator, including controls and safety devices, are in satisfactory operating condition. The requirements for prepurge and time between restarts referred to in 4.1 should be verified at the time of the installation test.

**7.3.1** *Flame safeguard.* The operation of the flame safeguard system should be verified by causing flame and ignition failures. Operation of the audible alarm (where applicable) and visible indicator should be verified. The shutdown times should be verified.

**7.3.2** *Limit controls.* Shutdown due to the operation of the limit controls should be verified.

**7.3.2.1** *Oil pressure limit control.* The lowering of the fuel oil pressure below the value required for safe combustion should initiate a safety shutdown.

**7.3.2.2** *Other interlocks.* Other interlocks provided should be tested for proper operation as specified by the unit manufacturer.

**7.3.3** *Combustion controls.* The combustion controls should be stable and operate smoothly.

**7.3.4** *Programming controls.* Programming controls should be verified as controlling and cycling the unit in the intended manner. Proper prepurge, ignition, postpurge, and modulation should be verified. A stopwatch should be used for verifying intervals of time.

**7.3.5** *Fuel supply controls.* The satisfactory operation of the two fuel control solenoid valves for all conditions of operation and shutdown should be verified.

**7.3.6.** *Low voltage test.* A low voltage test should be conducted on the incinerator unit to satisfactorily demonstrate that the fuel supply to the burners will be automatically shut off before an incinerator malfunction results from the reduced voltage.

**7.3.7** *Switches.* All switches should be tested to verify proper operation.

## 8 Certification

**8.1** Manufacturer's certification that an incinerator has been constructed in accordance with this standard should be provided (by letter, certificate, or in the instruction manual).

## 9 Marking

**9.1** Each incinerator should be permanently marked indicating:

**9.1.1** Manufacturer's name or trademark.

**9.1.2** Style, type, model or other manufacturer's designation for the incinerator.

**9.1.3** Capacity – to be indicated by net designed heat release of the incinerator in heat units per timed period; for example, British Thermal Units per hour, megajoules per hour, kilocalories per hour.

## 10 Quality assurance

Incinerators should be designed, manufactured and tested in a manner that ensures they meet the requirements of this standard.

## A1 Emission standard for shipboard incinerators with capacities of up to 1,500 kW

*Minimum information to be provided*

**A1.1** An IMO Type Approval Certificate should be required for each shipboard incinerator. In order to obtain such certificate, the incinerator should be designed and built to an IMO approved standard. Each model should go through a specified type approval test operation at the factory or an approved test facility, and under the responsibility of the Administration.

**A1.2** Type approval test should include measuring of the following parameters:

| | |
|---|---|
| Max capacity: | kW or kcal/h<br>kg/h of specified waste<br>kg/h per burner |
| Pilot fuel consumption: | kg/h per burner |
| $O_2$ average in combustion chamber/zone: | % |
| CO average in flue gas: | mg/MJ |
| Soot number average: | Bacharach or Ringelman scale |
| Combustion chamber flue gas outlet temperature average: | °C |
| Amount of unburned components in ashes: | % by weight |

**A1.3** *Duration of test operation*

| | |
|---|---|
| For sludge oil burning: | 6–8 hours |
| For solid waste burning: | 6–8 hours |

**A1.4** *Fuel/waste specification for type approval test (% by weight)*

| | |
|---|---|
| Sludge oil consisting of: | 75% sludge oil from heavy fuel oil<br>5% waste lubricating oil<br>20% emulsified water |
| Solid waste (class 2) consisting of: | 50% food waste<br>50% rubbish containing approx. 30% paper,<br>" 40% cardboard,<br>" 10% rags,<br>" 20% plastic<br>The mixture will have up to 50% moisture and 7% incombustible solids |

*Classes of waste*

Reference: Waste Classification from Incinerator Institute of America (Information for type approval tests only)

Class 2 Refuse, consisting of approximately even mixture of rubbish and garbage by weight. This type waste is common to passenger ships occupancy, consisting of up to 50% moisture, 7% incombustible solids and has a heating value of about 10,000 kJ/kg as fired.

| **Calorific values** | **kJ/kg** | **kcal/kg** |
|---|---|---|
| Vegetable and putrescibles | 5,700 | 1,360 |
| Paper | 14,300 | 3,415 |
| Rags | 15,500 | 3,700 |
| Plastics | 36,000 | 8,600 |
| Oil sludge | 36,000 | 8,600 |
| Sewage sludge | 3,000 | 716 |

| **Densities** | **$kg/m^3$** |
|---|---|
| Paper (loose) | 50 |
| Refuse (75% wet) | 720 |
| Dry rubbish | 110 |
| Scrap wood | 190 |
| Wood sawdust | 220 |

Density of loose general waste generated on board ship will be about 130 $kg/m^3$.

**A1.5** *Required emission standards to be verified by type approval test*

| | |
|---|---|
| $O_2$ in combustion chamber | 6–12% |
| CO in flue gas maximum average | 200 mg/MJ |
| Soot number maximum average | Bacharach 3 or Ringelman 1 (A higher soot number is acceptable only during very short periods such as starting up) |
| Unburned components in ash residues | Max 10% by weight |
| Combustion chamber flue gas outlet temperature range | 850–1200°C |

Flue gas outlet temperature and $O_2$ content should be measured during the combustion period, and not during the preheating or cooling periods. For a batch loaded incinerator, it is acceptable to carry out the type approval test by means of a single batch.

A high temperature in the actual combustion chamber/zone is an absolute requirement in order to obtain a complete and smoke free incineration, including that of plastic and other synthetic materials while minimizing dioxine, VOCs (volatile organic compounds), and emissions.

### **A1.6** *Fuel-related emission*

**A1.6.1** Even with good incineration technology the emission from an incinerator will depend on the type of material being incinerated. If for instance a vessel has bunkered a fuel with high sulphur content, then sludge oil from separators which is burned in the incinerator will lead to emission of $SO_x$. But again, the $SO_x$ emission from the incinerator would only amount to less than one per cent of the $SO_x$ discharged with the exhaust from main and auxiliary engines.

**A1.6.2** Principal organic constituents (POCs) cannot be measured on a continuous basis. Specifically, there are no instruments with provision for continuous time telemetry that measures POC, HCl, or waste destruction efficiency, to date. These measurements can only be made using grab sample approaches where the sample is returned to a laboratory for analysis. In the case of organic constituents (undestroyed wastes), the laboratory work requires considerable time to complete. Thus, continuous emission control can only be assured by secondary measurements.

**A1.6.3** On-board operation/emission control

For a shipboard incinerator with IMO type approval, emission control/monitoring should be limited to the following:

**.1** Control/monitor $O_2$ content in combustion chamber (spot checks only; an $O_2$ content analyser is not required to be kept on board).

**.2** Control/monitor temperature in combustion chamber flue gas outlet.

By continuous (auto) control of the incineration process, ensure that the above-mentioned two parameters are kept within the prescribed limits. This mode of operation will ensure that particulates and ash residue contain only traces of organic constituents.

### A1.7 *Passenger/cruise ships with incinerator installations having a total capacity of more than 1,500 kW*

**A1.7.1** On board this type of vessel, the following conditions will probably exist:

- **.1** Generation of huge amounts of burnable waste with a high content of plastic and synthetic materials.
- **.2** Incinerating plant with a high capacity operating continuously over long periods.
- **.3** This type of vessel will often be operating in very sensitive coastal areas.

**A1.7.2** In view of the fuel-related emission from a plant with such a high capacity, installation of a flue gas seawater scrubber should be considered. This installation can perform an efficient after-cleaning of the flue gases, thus minimizing the content of:

HCl
$SO_x$
Particulate matter

**A1.7.3** Any restriction on nitrogen oxide ($NO_x$) should only be considered in connection with possible future regulations on pollution from the vessel's total pollution, i.e., main and auxiliary machinery, boilers, etc.

## A2 Fire protection requirements for incinerators and waste stowage spaces

For the purpose of construction, arrangement and insulation, incinerator spaces and waste stowage spaces should be treated as category A machinery spaces (SOLAS II-2/3.31)* and service spaces, (SOLAS II-2/3.45), respectively. To minimize the fire hazards these spaces represent, the following SOLAS requirements in chapter II-2 should be applied:

* References have been updated for this publication to reflect amendments to SOLAS.

**A2.1** For passenger vessels carrying more than 36 passengers:

**.1** regulation 9.2.2.3.2.2(12) should apply to incinerator and combined incinerator/waste storage spaces, and the flue uptakes from such spaces; and

**.2** regulation 9.2.2.3.2.2(13) should apply to waste storage spaces and garbage chutes connected thereto.

**A2.2** For all other vessels including passenger vessels carrying not more than 36 passengers:

**.1** regulation 9.2.2.4.2.2(6) should apply to incinerator and combined incinerator/waste spaces, and the flue uptakes from such spaces; and

**.2** regulation 9.2.2.4.2.2(9) should apply to waste storage spaces and garbage chutes connected thereto.

**A2.3** Incinerators and waste storage spaces located on weather decks (regulation II-2/3.50) need not meet the above requirements but should be located:

**.1** as far aft on the vessel as possible;

**.2** not less than 3 m from entrances, air inlets and openings to accommodations, service spaces and control stations;

**.3** not less than 5 m measured horizontally from the nearest hazardous area, or vent outlet from a hazardous area; and

**.4** not less than 2 m should separate the incinerator and the waste material storage area, unless physically separated by a structural fire barrier.

**A2.4** A fixed fire detection and fire-extinguishing system should be installed in enclosed spaces containing incinerators, in combined incinerator/waste storage spaces, and in any waste storage space in accordance with the following table:

| | **Automatic sprinkler system** | **Fixed fire-extinguishing system** | **Fixed fire detection system** |
|---|---|---|---|
| Combined incinerator and waste storage space | X | | |
| Incinerator space | | X | X |
| Waste storage space | X | | |

**A2.5** Where an incinerator or waste storage space is located on weather decks it must be accessible with two means of fire extinguishment; either fire hoses, semi-portable fire extinguishers, fire monitors or combination of any two of these extinguishing devices. A fixed fire-extinguishing system is acceptable as one means of extinguishment.

**A2.6** Flue uptake piping/ducting should be led independently to an appropriate terminus via a continuous funnel or trunk.

### A3 Incinerators integrated with heat recovery units

**A3.1** The flue gas system, for incinerators where the flue gas is led through a heat recovery device, should be designed so that the incinerator can continue operation with the economizer coils dry. This may be accomplished with bypass dampers if needed.

**A3.2** The incinerator unit should be equipped with a visual and an audible alarm in case of loss of feed-water.

**A3.3** The gas-side of the heat recovery device should have equipment for proper cleaning. Sufficient access should be provided for adequate inspection of external heating surfaces.

### A4 Flue gas temperature

**A4.1** When deciding upon the type of incinerator, consideration should be given as to what the flue gas temperature will be. The flue gas temperature can be a determining factor in the selection of materials for fabricating the stack. Special high temperature material may be required for use in fabricating the stack when the flue gas temperatures exceed 430°C.

## Annex

*Form of IMO Type Approval Certificate for shipboard incinerators with capacities of up to 1,500 kW*

### CERTIFICATE OF SHIPBOARD INCINERATOR

NAME OF ADMINISTRATION

*BADGE*
*OR*
*CYPHER*

This is to certify that the shipboard incinerator listed has been examined and tested in accordance with the requirements of the Standard for Shipboard Incinerators for disposing of ship-generated waste appended to the Guidelines for the Implementation of Annex V of MARPOL 73/78 as amended by resolution MEPC.76(40) and referenced by regulation 16 of Annex VI to MARPOL 73/78.*

Incinerator manufactured by . . . . . . . . . . . . . . . . . . . . . . . . .

Style, type or model for the incinerator† . . . . . . . . . . . . . . . . . .

Max. capacity . . . . . . . . . . . . . . . . . kW or kcal/h
. . . . . . . . . . . . . . . . . kg/h of specified waste
. . . . . . . . . . . . . . . . . kg/h per burner

$O_2$ average
in combustion chamber/zone . . . . . %

CO average in flue gas . . . . . . . . . . mg/MJ

Soot number average . . . . . . . . . . . Bacharach or Ringelman scale

Combustion chamber flue gas
outlet temperature average . . . . . . . °C

Amount of unburned components
in ashes . . . . . . . . . . . . . . . . . . . . . % by weight

* The introductory paragraph is amended by resolution MEPC.93(45).

† Delete as appropriate.

A copy of this certificate should be carried on board a vessel fitted with this equipment at all times.

Signed . . . . . . . . . . . . . . . . . . . . . . . . . . . . . . . . . . . . . . . . . . .

Administration of . . . . . . . . . . . . . . . . . . . . . . . . . . . . . . . . . . . .

Dated this . . . . day of . . . . . . . . . . . . . . . . . . . . . . . . . . . 20 . . . .

Official stamp

## Future developments

**1** It should be observed that the following guidelines will be updated as a consequence of the revision of MARPOL Annex VI and the $NO_x$ Technical Code and, therefore, may be substantially changed. The work is expected to be finalized no later than MEPC 60 (March/April 2010):

- **.1** Guidelines for monitoring the worldwide average sulphur content of residual fuel oils supplied for use on board ships (resolution MEPC.82(43));
- **.2** Guidelines for the sampling of fuel oil for determination of compliance with MARPOL Annex VI (resolution MEPC.96(47));
- **.3** Survey Guidelines under the Harmonized System of Survey and Certification, 2007 (resolution A.997(25)) (see also resolution MEPC.128(53), Amendments to the revised survey guidelines under the Harmonized System of Survey and Certification); and
- **.4** Guidelines for port State control under MARPOL Annex VI (resolution MEPC.129(53)) and resolution A.787(19) on Procedures for port State control, as amended by resolution A.882(21).

**2** It should also be observed that the following guidelines will be developed under the revised MARPOL Annex VI and are expected to be finalized no later than MEPC 60:

- **.1** Guidelines for replacement engines not required to meet the Tier III limit, as required under regulation 13.2.2;
- **.2** Guidelines for the development of a VOC management plan, as required under regulation 15.6; and
- **.3** Guidelines on the provision of reception facilities, as required by regulation 17.

**3** It should further be observed that Guidelines for approval of $NO_x$-reducing devices by on-board testing, as required by paragraph 2.2.5.6 of the $NO_x$ Technical Code 2008, will be developed, and are expected to be finalized no later than MEPC 60.

**4** When finalized and adopted by the MEPC, the above-listed guidelines, or relevant parts thereof, together with other information associated with the revised MARPOL Annex VI and the $NO_x$ Technical Code 2008, will be issued as a separate publication. It may be noted that, as regards the guidelines listed in paragraphs 1.3 and 1.4 above, the 26th session of the IMO Assembly, in November/ December 2009, will consider and adopt the revised versions of these sets of guidelines.

# Notes

# Notes

# Notes

# Notes

# Notes

# Notes